EPIGRAMS AND CRITICISMS IN MINIATURE

Epigrams and Criticisms in Miniature

By WILLIAM LAURENCE SULLIVAN

Feror exsul in altum

Philadelphia
UNIVERSITY OF PENNSYLVANIA PRESS

London: Humphrey Milford
Oxford University Press

1936

Manufactured in the United States of America

Estellae Dilectissimae
Hoc opusculum indignum
In pignus amoris
Dedicat
Auctor.

Biographical Sketch

GENTLE, modest Joanna Desmon smiled a quiet smile as she looked at the little bundle of humanity in the arms of her husband, Patrick Sullivan. He was holding their second child, William, born on that bleak fifteenth of November, 1872, at East Braintree, Massachusetts, far from the lovely Irish town of Bandon from which she and Patrick had come only the year before. But neither he nor she dreamed that his arms sheltered one whose extraordinary gifts of mind and heart were to claim for him a place among the intellectual and spiritual leaders of his time.

The boy showed early a love for books, and at the age of five read the *Lives of the Saints* and was so filled with fervor that he then chose the name of the martyr Laurence as the name that should become his at confirmation. His parents were Roman Catholics, but while attentive to their duties as such, neither of them was a *devoté*. His mother, gentle to a remarkable degree, was yet inflexible in any matter involving principle. His father was full of impetuous enthusiasm, but he died when the boy was only fourteen and the lad grew into manhood under the guidance of his mother.

The family had moved to Quincy in William's infancy, and so it was in the public schools there that he began his student life. He made rapid progress in his studies and excelled in athletics, especially baseball. From the Quincy High School he went to Boston College and to St. John's Seminary in Brighton (Boston). He was distinguished in English and the classics, winning in his second year at the Seminary the coveted Fulton medal in public debate. Two years later, in 1896, he received the degree of Ph.B. and in 1899 and 1900 the degrees of S.T.B. and S.T.L. from the Catholic University of America. To these Meadville Theological

School (Unitarian) added a D.D. in 1917, and Temple University of Philadelphia in 1934 an LL.D.

Following a decision made in boyhood, he was ordained to the Roman Catholic priesthood in 1899, became a member of the Paulist community, a congregation of missionaries especially to non-Catholics, and remained with them until May 1909. During several years of that period he was professor of Sacred Scripture and Theology at St. Thomas's College (Catholic University). While teaching he became interested in the Modernist Movement then gathering strength among the Catholic clergy of both Europe and America. Despite valiant efforts to retain his belief in the dogmas of the ancient faith, he was constrained by the strength of his convictions to withdraw from the Catholic Church two years before Pope Pius X issued the encyclical against Modernism. At the time of his retirement he was pastor of a Paulist church near the University of Texas in Austin.

His mother, whom he deeply loved, had died just before his ordination. As there were no family ties and he wished not to influence his friends and former students by his decision, he withdrew to Kansas City, Missouri. There for two years he remained in great loneliness and considerable privation, as he had no income except what he could earn by occasional writing for magazines and newspapers.

Through one of his devoted younger friends he left Kansas City in the autumn of 1910 for Cleveland, Ohio, where he engaged in tutoring for several months. While there he joined the Unitarian Church, having found in James Martineau a spiritual companionship. His stay in Cleveland was brief, however, as he accepted an invitation to teach English and history in the Ethical Culture School of New York City in 1911–12. But as his whole soul was centred in religious and spiritual matters he could not long remain satisfied in other work. Accordingly in October 1912, he entered the Unitarian Fellowship for the Ministry, and became pastor of the struggling church of All Souls, Schenectady, New York.

It was not long before his brilliant preaching and consecrated personality attracted wide attention. As a result he was called to the associate pastorate of All Souls' Church, New York City. He accepted the call on the condition that he might carry on for at least a year the work in Schenectady. During this double ministry he gave many lectures and addresses, so many indeed that his health, never robust, necessitated a leave of absence for several months in 1915. But the next year saw him on a mission for the American Unitarian Association to the Pacific Coast, where in the month of September he preached more than forty sermons.

In 1917 he was the Dudleian lecturer at Harvard.

By 1922 All Souls' Church, of which Dr. Sullivan had become pastor in 1916, had celebrated the hundredth anniversary of its founding and paid its entire indebtedness. He therefore felt free to accept the urgent invitation of the Unitarian Laymen's League to become Mission-Preacher to the United States. The two years spent in this work were exhausting, but so fruitful that he did not regret the expenditure of his strength. At the end of the second year he resigned in order to give himself to writing.

But this was not yet to be. The Church of the Messiah, St. Louis, Missouri, was in need of a pastor and Dr. Sullivan yielded to their insistence, expecting to remain there three months. He stayed, however, four years. During the summer of his first year in St. Louis he taught in the Meadville Theological School (University of Chicago) and during his entire stay in the West he gave an incredible number of lectures and addresses. Had he been obliged to write his speeches he could not have made half of them, but from a well-stored mind he drew a wealth of material with which to clothe his thought once he had his pattern, and spoke extemporaneously with an English diction not often equaled.

In 1928 he withdrew to Mt. Gretna, Pennsylvania, again hoping to devote himself to writing, but calls for sermons and lectures found their way without interruption to his "Nido," and after a year and a half he accepted the unanimous call of the Unitarian Society of Germantown, Pennsylvania. In December 1929 he took up his ministry there, and remained in the happiest association with that congregation until his death, October 5, 1935.

In 1913 Dr. Sullivan married Estelle Throckmorton, the daughter of Hugh William and Rebecca Ellen (Upton) Throckmorton of Virginia, who survives him.

He was a member of the Authors Club of New York, of the Union League and the Phi Alpha (a Ministers' Association) of Philadelphia, and of the Science and Arts and the Informal Club of Germantown.

It is not surprising that in a life so filled with speaking and traveling Dr. Sullivan should have had little time for writing. But he did publish *Letters to His Holiness, Pius X,* 1910; *The Priest,* 1912; *From the Gospel to the Creeds,* 1919; *Readings for Meditation: First Series,* 1922, *Second Series,* 1935. Two articles of his in the *Atlantic Monthly:* "Our Spiritual Destitution," March 1929, and "The Anti-Religious Front," January 1930, were widely read and quoted. For six years he reviewed books for the New York *Herald-Tribune.* In addition to his published work he left a few chapters of an autobiography, and enough verse of depth and power to fill a small volume.

One of the extraordinary features of Dr. Sullivan's relation with other denominations than the Unitarian may be mentioned—they called on him to speak, to preach, to conduct retreats for their ministers, even for their theological students, as if he belonged to all of them. In fact, the last service he rendered outside his own church was giving a retreat for Congregational ministers in September 1935.

His brilliant mind, his devout spiritual nature, his keen sense of humor, his great eloquence compounded of all these, his charity toward all in thought and deed, and his modest opinion of his own attainments endeared him to all with whom he came in contact. The old found him tender and full of courtesy, the young were sure of his understanding sympathy and yielded him a sincere admiration and a pure devotion, while the poor dwelt in his heart.

E. T. S.

Author's Foreword

Two reflections disturb an author who writes a book of epigrams. One is that his terseness may be triteness; that his little cartridge of thought may lack the powder of wit and insight and so when the trigger is pressed may merely make a verbal click but shoot out no bullet of wisdom. Alas! there is no exorcising this spectre; and one's only consolation is—unworthy enough, I know—that there are so many such ineffectual ghosts between book covers already that the addition of one more cannot seriously add to the terrors of literature.

The other disturbing reflection is that in complete innocence one may have said something that has been said before. There are cracks in the mind that let in everything but light, and through one of these fissures that slippery conveyancer, the subconscious mind, may push in a maxim encountered long ago in Joubert, let us say, or Goethe or Landor, and palm it off as original. It is a terrible thought, and I will not invoke upon it the threadbare anathema: *Pereant qui ante nos nostra dixerunt,* but only profess penitence in advance for the possible transgression, and assure my readers—if it is any good to do so—that I have not deliberately filched a ray from anybody's halo. And so, not without quaking from both apprehensions, I send out these epigrams to receive their predestined epinicion or epitaph.

W. L. S.

Contents

EPIGRAMS

1. Society and Institutions

THE Parliament of Man is in mad disorder because the Sovereign's chair is vacant.

We are willing enough to repent; but the Higher Law requires that we expiate.

Fools and sages—says Goethe—are not dangerous; but half-fools and half-sages are.

A growing number of gentlemen in black gowns, long accustomed to the war of creeds, are busy inciting the gentlemen of red principles who are fiercely preparing the war of classes. The modern militant cleric smells a fight as far off as his more orthodox predecessors smelt heresy. But he is aware all the time of the immunity of his profession. He knows that if bloody battles come the responsibility and the reproach will be laid upon personages more important; and if grievous wounds are to be borne, the suffering will be undergone by men less privileged.

When the hour of the Dictator strikes his country snores on.

A terrible thought comes to mind concerning the earthly Paradise promised us by our sociological fortune-tellers. Perhaps there would be armed angels at the gate to prevent anybody from getting out!

In state and church, as in philosophy and psychology, men of sharp sight have a remarkable liability to dull vision.

Ours is an age which may well say: "I am dying of the diseases of my doctors."

Just as we make the discovery that the flaming demon of the millennial has been ruining our religion, we call in the lying legion of the visionary to save our democracy.

When a great leader dies he leaves a people strengthened. When a demagogue or a dictator dies he leaves a population coarsened.

The detached and dilettante social philosopher may believe that history is a series of cycles. The shaggy moralist insists that it is a series of cyclones.

Give the public what they want? The surest way of making them want the heads of their benefactors for not giving them something else!

Every leader of men should be a terrestrial pessimist and a cosmic optimist. Unless he is the former he will have a broken heart at the end; unless he is the latter he will have a murky vision from the beginning.

Those whose name is Legion have a surname, and it is Majority.

Democracies have shallow and noisy passions; therefore deep and secret fears.

History is the record of new corruptions growing from the grave of old retributions.

Britain is slow in rising; we are swift in falling.

When a nation arrives at its most tragic hour its stage is crowded with comedians. They are killed off in the last act.

Ambitious and arbitrary persons in high station strengthen their power for the moment but weaken their office forever.

The advantage of long-tested institutions is that they provide experience ready-made. The trouble with hasty reforms is that they offer programmes recently dreamt.

We are sunk in sentimentalism if we refuse to recognize that states are prepared to commit any atrocity of crime if it is likely to pay, and that men in the mass are ready to approve any infamy of iniquity if it promises to be profitable.

The fatal fault of democracy is that it forbids the leaders of its policies to rise above the level of its passions.

Vox populi, vox Dei: but perhaps oftener, nox Dei!

The executioners of self-government are ungoverned selves.

When men are recovering from the debauch of anarchy they call for a stiff drink of old Authority.

When men cease to make glorious poetry of their hopes, they will make hellish prose of their despair.

Not in the deep sands of Time does History bury its mistakes and stupidities, but in a much safer oblivion—the shallow memories of men.

When her grown children become too big to be spanked, yet too perverse to be tolerated, Mother Nature hands them over for chastisement to Father Destiny, who is all moodiness and muscle and has no trace whatever of a heart.

Dwell too long on the basest men of history and you lose your hope. Live intimately with the noblest and you imperil your peace.

The course of history is the endeavor of men to catch up with Man.

A great deal of human history consists of the conflict between enlightenment and Light.

In an age of Faith there is Fear. In an age of no-Faith there is Fright.

Man has an abiding fear of being struck by enlightening.

The question is: Shall America perish before it substitutes culture for schooling?

There is no greater aphorism than Landor's: "When little men cast long shadows it is a sign that the sun is setting."

As the Secret Grand Lodge of the Sons of Splendor parade down the main street of Smearsburg, girt with sashes and swords, wearing velvet doublets and satin breeches, and with tasseled beanpots upside down on their heads—grocers in the panoply of crusaders, undertakers in the rig of mediaeval condottieri, coal-feed-and-hay merchants brave with the glory of Pretorian Guards—the intelligentsia give to the winds of heaven their howls of derision. Voilà, America's booberie en marche! But straightway these intelligentsia announce with fearful seriousness that they themselves constitute "the civilized minority," that they are our "mature minds," our "adult few," our "intellectuals," and our "lonely advance guard of modernity"! And not one echo do they catch of the crashing laughter of the spectators in the Higher Spheres!

Dictatorships die of concentrated arrogance; democracies, of organized appetite.

Behind the scenes in the drama of History there is a prompter named Experience. The leading actors often have him dismissed because his corrections are so constant that they interrupt the farce.

Drink the cup of the Fathers, but give the pledge to the Living.

We need an unearthly faith if we are to be made fit to live upon the earth.

Caliban said of Trinculo and Stephano: "What a thrice-double ass was I to take this drunkard for a god and worship this dull fool!" We have had Caliban's experience; now to share his insight and indignation!

A good many people fancy themselves bold pagans because they believe in Chance; whereas if they had the hardihood to be real pagans they would believe in Nemesis.

Materialism in the School implies despotism in the State.

To-day the worst traitors to Liberty are to be found among the advocates of liberalism.

Civilization is in peril? Put it correctly. Civilization *is* peril! The higher it rises the more unstable its hold and the more disastrous its fall. Its safety consists in increasing the peril and going on up.

The crimes of history are never redeemed by repentance. They are punished—and how dreadfully!—by making additional crimes inevitable.

Inducing us to love other peoples by studying their history is one of the queerest notions that ever entered a human head. We must love them in spite of their history!

There are creatures who call it progress when people who once were taught magnificence in simple words come to be taught insignificance in big words.

Civilization in its decrepitude passes from the faith of the ardent and the endurance of the heroic to the notions, the schemes, and the systems of the sedentary.

A tragic view of life is the only solid foundation for Optimism. A jaunty view of life is the certain precursor of Pessimism.

It is a bad sign for the culture of an age to see fancies grow exciting and Fancy dull.

Americans have been an exploiting people, never a generously adventuring or an imaginatively pioneering one. They have brusquely conquered rather than spiritually assimilated their frontier. All the pathos, most of the forlorn heroism, and nearly the whole of the dramatic splendor of our advance upon the wilderness are centred upon the primitive peoples whom we dispossessed, and the beautiful flowers of ancient myth and ritual upon which we set our iron boots. Crush and then pity! has been our confused creed. It expresses the sentimentality of the heartless; the virtue-varnish of the unenlightened and unloving; the contrition-principle of the impenitent who paradoxically cannot rid themselves of remorse.

Bombings, lynchings, train-wreckings, kidnapings, professional killers bidding for business and clients in plenty to hire them! If hell, as they say, has ceased to be a belief, perhaps it is because it has become indubitable fact.

The illiterate never destroyed a state or a civilization till clever corrupters put it into their minds and taught them how to do it.

A useful chapter in social history might be headed: "The harmlessness of the illiterate when let alone, and the danger of the clever if left alone."

Politicians in a democracy ask not what questions are too important to neglect, but what questions are too hot to handle.

Men have from time to time proposed the axiom: "No work, no bread!" But no man has ever dared to threaten the calamity of "No thought, no talk!"

The next to the last downward step in a dying society is government by clowns. The very last is government by clowns accepted by slaves.

How often the historic sumptuousness of an institution is invoked in order to hide the present poverty of its ministrations!

Just as self-government throughout the world is proving too high for mature man we introduce it into the kindergarten. Unfortunately it is the mature men who have proved unfit for it that supervise and expound it in the kindergarten.

There is no loneliness like the loneliness of liberty. Liberty requires to be dedicated to a Cause which it binds itself to love, honor, and obey.

We are not pedestrians let loose for a constitutional before our long night's sleep. We are sentinels pacing our round for the protection of the ark of the Covenant, the tables of the Law, the sanctuary of the Fathers, and the banner of the King.

The fall of democracies is as frequent as the fall of dynasties. On the same slippery slope, near together, if not holding hands, stand democrats and despots.

In a poll involving a contest between the lasting good of our country and the immediate profit of our gang, the counting of the votes for the latter will soon take us into five figures; for the former we shall need hardly more than five fingers.

Do not look for decency in a democracy. Do not look for refinement in schools. Do not look for wisdom in philosophy. Do not look for candor in churches. Then with this insight gained, equip yourself to find all these priceless things in the sequestered place that gives them sanctuary.

When an age is in the last stage of decadence it cannot achieve sublimity even in its sins, and cannot avoid imposture even in its despair.

An age is irredeemably rotten when it regards nothing as so frivolous as fidelity and nothing so incredible as innocence.

Englishmen may be superior and arrogant when they discourse upon their Empire. But they become beings actually beautiful when their reverent voices speak of the Head of their Empire.

Never despise the common people! Give them the wistful love that every man must feel for the misled. If contemptuousness is so strong within you that you must find some outlet for it, bestow it upon the charlatans of necromancy who promise the common people an easy millennium, upon the corrupters who infect them in the name of learning, and upon the faithless shepherds who let them die destitute under the invocation of religion.

The Nature that abhors a vacuum can hardly be expected to bless with success the efforts of the politicians, pedagogues, and philosophers who are trying to pull something substantial out of a vacuum.

From unity to unit, from aggregation to individuation, from dependence to independence, from protection to peril, from "we" to "I"—this is the rhythm of progress and perfection. The tragic feature of the advance is that the emancipated human unit carries over into his new freedom the grossness, the despotism, the inert dumbness and monotonous dullness of the matrix-mass.

For the sake of our generation's amour propre we regret that modernity is often described by its zealots as if it required our preferring the croaking of frogs and the bellowing of unclean buffaloes to the music of undying voices and the singing of woodland thrush.

Civilized man corresponds to what evolutionists call a mutant type—a precarious departure from the usual course and traditional habit-pattern of the species. Only one thing preserves mutant forms—rigorous breeding. Without that the mutant returns to the wild.

The spiritual insight of our age has been perverted by an abstraction called Matter paraded in the name of Science, and by an aberration called economic materialism given by Socialism the title of a faith and the title-deed to a Millennium.

Britain remains the chief sanctuary of Freedom. The time may come in the United States when an advocate of Liberty will be accused of speaking with an English accent.

To the same music the Seer departs and the Avenger enters.

History has the necessity of tragedy. The fifth act, which is of expiation, other ages have seen before the final curtain fell for them. We have watched the play into the fourth act, which is the climax of boastful foolishness and arrogant perversity, but we do not remember yet how it always ends.

Do not turn on the light of Spirit too suddenly. It might show us that our banquet is of husks and our companionship with pigs.

The spirit of History is sad, not because it contemplates the heaped ruins of time, but because we insist upon adding ourselves to the heap.

If our educational psychologists continue their dictatorship much longer, our most venerable institution may be called: the little-read schoolhouse.

Americans do not greatly care for learning. But they mischievously delight in making the charlatan believe that they like to be bamboozled learnedly.

"I have a right to anybody else's property!" That is the principle of a thief. "I have a right to everybody else's property!" That is the principle of a grand reform which promises the millennium and receives the blessing of a large number of pulpiteering moralists!

To be gregarious is for geese, sheep, buffaloes, and bacteria. To be anti-gregarious is absolutely imposed upon Persons grown up to independence and responsibility.

If ever we are sane enough to be happy once more, how we shall shake the world with laughter at the experts and specialists to whom we gave the custody of our fortunes, our minds, our country, and our souls!

Forlorn philosopher, are you teaching the higher life? But some obese clown in Hollywood is preparing a putrid picture that will teach life-lessons to a hundred thousand for every pupil you have. But keep straight on! Those are ever the normal odds against truth and decency.

There have always been human beings without reverence, without courtesy, without restraint, without taste. But only now have they been produced scientifically and by pedagogical methods.

In this country to-day there is less danger that the rich will become oppressors than that the not-rich will become thieves.

If the stall-fed earthly millennium now so fervently preached at us should come to pass, men would return to belief in hell in order to bring back into life some imaginative magnificence and some sense of heroic peril.

There is one thing a dictator must never do—he must not make himself ridiculous. He may only make his country ridiculous.

Capitalism is dying. Therefore, says the Socialist, let us try a system that has never been alive.

Europeans have become tetchy and jumpy. They have lost their good nature. Jacques Bonhomme, for example, is now gone sour and is totally destitute of bonhomie. But Uncle Sam still wears a grin, doesn't care who steals his money, and wonders why somebody has not stolen the little that he has not squandered.

The explainers are many, a large and noisy army, and we cannot escape them. The interpreters are few and reticent, and we have to hunt them out.

America is trying to convince itself that it has a future to live for while infecting itself with the diseases that all past republics have died of.

Americans proclaim their wickedness vociferously through headlines and megaphones. As a consequence shocked Europeans profess to regard us as on a cultural and moral level with Iroquois and Apaches. These Europeans themselves are more genteel and discreet. They put on evening dress and whisper their sins in the hushed privacy of the confessional—having first made sure that the Father-confessor is hard of hearing.

Democracy places a senseless hope on the equality of man. Its only possible foundation is the quality of Man.

In our age of transition it is more dangerous that we are ignorant of what we are abandoning than that we do not know where we are going.

If ever the modern world is to have a great culture the roots of it cannot possibly grow in a soil so thin, dry, and sandy as that of the schools. They must draw nourishment from the dark and deep-lying earth of our profoundest souls. They must grow from a spiritual experience too vital for even academic dandyism and dilettanteism to kill.

It is sad when the blind lead the blind; but immeasurably sadder is the spectacle of the servile multitudes who insist upon being blinded in order to be led.

Americans have a liking for the iconoclast, praise him, and with copious cash reward him. But when the hammer-wielding is ended and he has passed by, they put back upon pedestals the images which he has defaced.

Sir Jabesh Windbag and Viscount Mealymouth are inventions of Carlyle's Titanic scorn. He took a Titan's joy in pummeling them. But for all his good-will he could not give them their quietus. Not only do they live, they are telling us how to live and what to believe. They are even writing the charter of the sociological millennium, and the firm's name, Windbag and Mealymouth, is lettered in brass over the gates of that pot-bellied Paradise.

Unless you become as little children in these days you will probably not know the names of the heroes of Hollywood nor the sex-adventures of its heroines.

If civilization is to go under let it be from the shaggy despot rather than from the diseased decadent!

The analphabetically illiterate are only a problem. The learned illiterate are a peril.

Our iconoclastic biographers believe that there is a rule of thumb for understanding great men. It consists in applying the thumb of the extended hand to the tip of one's nose.

The first impulse of the politician, civil or ecclesiastical, is to gain a point by manoeuvre, to cover a design with subtlety, to promote a plan by deviousness, to advance a scheme by slippery artifice, and under protestations of high honor to sink a stiletto into Truth. A truth-teller, a man who will not use the backstairs, a despiser of chambered conspiracies, and a hater of lies, whether the lies are naked or venerably robed—if there be such a man let him seek the companionship of the great dead; for in church and state there is no privacy so completely Carthusian as his.

How much easier it is to write a ton of books on pedagogy than to produce one teacher of sensitive structure, noble manner, and fine taste, whose essential presence and inward habit are a constant dissuasive to vulgarity and a living recommendation of the beauty of learning and the dignity of wisdom!

A radical defect in American education is that it is busy with our higher nurture but not concerned at all for our higher nature.

It is alarmingly frequent in history that a giant state produces dwarfs, and a dwarf state, giants. What counts most in a country is not the extent of its acreage but the spaciousness of its sky.

The universe utters discourse. It is the disaster of a frivolous age to imagine that the utterance is not eternal but extempore.

Americanism resembles the churches. There is more of ritual and recited piety toward the early Fathers and Founders than of loyalty to their principles.

Hitting empty souls with the club of pedantry constitutes the marching music of a decadent age.

The next generation dies in convulsions caused by the poison which the preceding generation found sweet.

It is not our fall that measures the extent of our decadence; it is what we fall from.

With a swarm of fantastic reforms being every day suggested in higher education, perhaps we may propose one as fantastic as any other, namely, that no man be taken into a learned faculty who is not in some rudimentary sense a gentleman, and even on the way to becoming a cultured gentleman.

If you would know on how thin a crust civilization stands, suppose the authoritative announcement to be made that for twenty-four hours all banks should be unguarded, with their deposit boxes unlocked and their vaults open. Suppose further that for this length of time the police should be deprived of power and courts suspended, and that no one should be held answerable for anything he might do that day. What havoc and hell would fill the day's history let the imagination picture if it dares. Yet doubtless on the following Sunday there would be preachers in plenty sermonizing on the "divinity of man," precisely as if that apotheosis required no more than that a biped should have a human form and face and walk about in breeches or a skirt!

With churches and states the heart becomes weak as the right arm grows strong.

Two uprooted men are acting with power upon To-day and will act more mightily upon Tomorrow: Friedrich Nietzsche, the ruined Christian, and Karl Marx, the ruined Jew. Nietzsche, the son of a minister, abhorred the mob; Marx, the descendant of rabbis, despised the individual. They are symbols of a choice that the twentieth century will have to make—portents of a fatality already amid vast rumblings dark upon the horizon of destiny. They are extremists both; but brilliant Nietzsche in his insane excess fascinates, while Marx in his leaden, morose, and humorless order repels. Nietzsche it would not be difficult to re-baptize. Marx it would be impossible to un-circumcise.

The daring prayer to turn stones to bread may be sometimes answered. The perverse petition to turn our bread to stone is unfailingly answered.

Primitive peoples build their history out of their Imagination. Creative ages build their imagination out of their history. A decadent era has for its first and radical curse paralysis of the imagination; so to make all things even it vilifies its history.

In the world of spirit it is the forlorn hope that is brilliant with the countenances of the hopeful.

Irreverence is not a mark of the barbarian. The barbarian is never irreverent. It is the mark of the civilized who have not risen to a barbarian's decency.

Liberty married Democracy in order to reform him. But his heart is with his old trull, Dame Despotism, and only his speeches are for Liberty, a windy offering which she is too proud to accept and too disillusioned to believe. Since the reform looks impossible, divorce seems inevitable.

A politician in a democracy may once in a rare while be found who will confess: "I was mistaken!" But the democratic politician still awaits discovery who will say to his electorate: "You were mistaken!" Democracy counsels discretion toward susceptibilities rather than valor in veracities.

The traditionalist guides the course of life and events by dead reckoning; the romanticist by the light still lingering from stars long extinguished; the radical by stars inside his own head produced by a collision with reality.

The thinker, the student, the scrupulous seeker, only gropes after certainty. The unmistakable mark of the demagogue is that he monopolizes it.

We are trying now to cultivate in people the experience of age by the experiments of juvenility, connoisseurship in sin without the inconvenience of remorse, the gratification of impulse without the burden of responsibility, and the possession of culture without the costliness of study. It is a programme for second-rate conjurers; and Destiny, though tolerant of many illusions, is very harsh in retribution upon illusionists.

The finale of boasting is whining.

The chieftain of a state who plans deliberate despotism may after all be less dangerous than a ruler who instead of principles in his head has only a series of casual seizures of happy thoughts.

In a capitalist society the dispossessed may indulge the dream of possession. Communism would not allow them even the possession of the dream.

Man devises an aristocracy of station; Nature decrees an aristocracy of status.

There is this serious misgiving concerning democracy, that as men learn to enjoy independence they grow to detest responsibility.

It takes generations of great believers to produce brazen and impenitent infidels. In America we have not quite the background for a convincing type of pagan. Our dalliers of heathenism caress their wanton either with the shamefaced feeling that somebody is looking or with a vulgar insolence which genuine heathenism never knew.

Primitive man is the permanent man—a fact which experienced demagogues remember and advanced theologians forget.

A proletariat which is purchased by the pauperizing largess of a demagogue government is an anomaly in transactions: it is the owner of its owner.

A managed economy has become a necessity. But who will manage the economists is a question that causes all the old ghosts to walk and all the old goblins to grin.

Liberalism despite its founders and first principles has acquired a lurch to despotism. Rationalism despite its saintly name betrays an affinity for Sensualism.

The hardest trial of the advocates of liberty comes not from sceptred tyrants forever alert but from the somnolent mob who have grown comfortably calloused in their chains.

There will be discord on earth till men love the same thing. There will be hell on earth till they know what they ought to love.

One monotonously repeated lesson of history is the blockheadedness of the brilliant.

A loose grasp upon principles is the immediate precursor of loose principles.

For nations there is no second childhood; but there may be imbecility of the overgrown head and the fantastic juvenility of the senile heart.

Wise and deep doctors of civilization may tell an age what is the matter with it. But it is the quacks who write the prescription and administer the medicine.

Persuasion by free discussion, but with accepted decencies above all opinions and with one loyalty supreme over all differences, is Britain's predestinate mark of election and salvation.

What facts of life and history are the most important? Those that man tries hardest not to see!

Demos is an animal that kills every Redeemer who tries to save him, and mangles every trainer who endeavors to tame him.

One of the unacknowledged and unspoken petitions of men in a decadent age is: Grant us the name, the prestige, and the dignity of Truth; but save us from the rigor, the particularity, and the responsibility of Truthfulness!

For the state and for individuals the inevitable end of squandering is stealing.

There is one monarch, and only one, whose history is unrelieved iniquity, half-bestial, half-insane, and his name is Mob.

As soon as Democracy becomes conscious of the brute power of its majorities it begins to destroy the spiritual authority of its principles.

Many a dignitary, civil, ecclesiastical, and academic, finds it his hardest work to live up to his title and his uniform.

Military unity, imperialistic unity, papal unity, national unity, commercial unity—all have broken under the hammer of Chaos because the artificers were not wise enough to understand the nature of the fundamental unit, which is the spirit of man. We must accept the terms of Chaos and crown Havoc as King unless we establish a spiritual unity absolutely dominated by the insight of Soul. Chaos and Havoc tremble at the thought; their servile disciples, our clever, learned, and otherwise benighted men of pomp and circumstance shake with laughter at it.

In most debatable questions put to the convocation of mankind the "I's" have it.

A cause may be won by the battles it has fought with its own supporters.

The plunderers organized for lifting public funds sing an old refrain upon one word of which they put significant emphasis: "It's always fair weather when good fellows *get* together."

Tom, Dick, and Harry are likable and friendly human beings so long as in a normal manner they walk the streets beside us and meet us in comradely equality. But Tom, Dick, and Harry incorporated, constituting a state that bosses us about or a proletarian dictatorship that boots us about, are the unpleasantest animals that could harass the mind or oppress the soul of man.

Dictators grow suddenly to mighty stature because Liberty has long been dying inch by inch.

Quiescence in corruption prepares for the onset of the murder-mania called Mob.

God's country! Be careful; you may find yourself in that sublimity of lonely wilderness!

In history there is no movement forward without movement upward; nor any movement downward that is not also backward.

In international utterances our country is an anomaly: it is evangelistic but with no sense of sin; millennial but with no conception of judgment; ardently believing that heaven is near but resolutely ignoring that hell is still nearer.

Thought-destroying fury is the enthusiasm of fanatics; conscience-murdering insanity the fanaticism of mobs.

De-spiritualize education and you de-vitalize life.

Arguments submitted to Reason haven't much chance against propaganda addressed to the spleen and promises offered to the belly.

The soldier's honor is crowned with a halo of immemorial romance. While churchmen have been devious, statesmen crooked, merchants cunning, and philosophers weak, the soldier has kept a high and lonely station as the servant of costly duty and loyalty unstained. He has been an anchorite living austerely and owning little, but rich in impractical and priceless honor. To shatter this chivalrous tradition is a distinction reserved for the United States. Our soldiers, their wars ended, charge upon the nation for privilege and lucre. In vain Presidents warn them that they are endangering the country's solvency and credit and degrading its dignity. As well might sheep warn wolves that they are endangering the flock. The cash though it involve ruin! greed though it shame a people! is the battle-cry of our legions. So on our inhospitable soil Honor takes off a uniform, as long ago it laid by mitre and ermine and frockcoat. Somewhere it still walks the lonely ways of the world, in rags and hopeless of companionship, but dreaming upon what memories, evoking what ghosts of chivalries forever gone!

A despot, like a believer in old Mithraism, regards himself as only half-initiated till he has a bath of blood.

Petulant rebels should remember that it is not by buttoning up a hot cinder of revolt inside his breeches that a man becomes Promethean.

In an age without faith it is the Winners who die of defeatism.

A materialist age does not hurt the world by preserving the unfit. It ruins the world by degrading the fit.

Many men argue that authority is the safeguard of liberty. But they fail to see the proper province of authority until they also admit that it is the servant of liberty.

The liberty of the individual is the greatest gift of God: the annihilation of the individual is the worst perversity of man.

The head of a state should not be voluble. Reticence is the most becoming garment of majesty; and when either a god or a president grows talkative he is lowered into gusty commonplace, and approaches the end of his prestige. The old Romans had a good rule about it:
Nec deus intersit nisi dignus vindice nodus
Inciderit. Let august beings attend only to august business!

The small things of the past which we recall in our individual memory are always wistfully enchanting. The heroic presences evoked in our national memory are always austerely reproachful.

There are men so ablaze with revolutionary fervor that they will probably accept no heaven hereafter except a spinning orbit, or a seat on the tail of a comet, and empty space to be made reverberant with declamation.

Man has enough of good in him to create a just and beautiful civilization every so often, and enough of evil to wreck it only too often.

In this one of our humble sayings let us be homiletic; America is in need of teachers who will train us how to be strong without being dirty; how to be independent without being clownish; how to be acute in mind without being barbarous in taste and shallow in soul.

Weep not! Before the little space of three hundred years is ended the blasphemies and pomposities, the imposture and corruption that shout through this desolate hour will have been covered with predestined dust and sunken in the oblivion of Lethean silence. Let us have joy! Souls will still live and will aspire, adore, and defy. Their brave portion will be what it ever is—felicities undarkened by any doom, loyalties untouched by decay, fulfilments with lifted spears and streaming banners driving into darkness the routed phantasms of decadence and despair!

As an instrument of peace and justice the League of Nations has pretty completely failed. But why speak of failure? The League was never meant to be an instrument of peace and justice. It was meant to preserve a status quo which was thoroughly to the liking of the nations victorious in the war. Desperately and gluttonously practical those nations were and are; and if they could induce a concert of states to guarantee the preservation of their opulence naturally they would make the association of guarantors the foundation of their public policy, as they humorously put it. And the Americans who describe them as noble countries working with chaste zeal for peace on earth and good will to men, and say that we for not joining them fall short of their virtue, are victims of a generous but monstrous delusion. What it seems impossible to get into our haunted heads is that there is no such thing in nations as disinterested virtue, no such standard of statesmanship as unselfish idealism, no such authority recognized in politics, in Socialism, in Communism, or in churches as a pure Sovereignty of Right binding equally all public groups and all private souls. Cash value is this world's law, and this world's ruin; and the aureole of perfection cannot be made to fit the swollen head of any corporation now existing or for a long time likely to exist upon our scene of sin.

We learn from edifying tradition certain great phrases illustrating the spirit of the Republic. "Give me liberty or give me death"; "Eternal vigilance is the price of liberty"; "Life, liberty, and the pursuit of happiness"; "Government of the people, for the people, and by the people"; and two or three more. But one clamorous cry in our resounding day has smothered them all: "Give us the cash!"

Liberty asks for your Spirit as a sanctuary; the omnipotent state for your Soul as a sacrifice.

Monarchies go down the road of ruin misled by the despotic. Hard upon their heels follow democracies bewitched by the eccentric.

2. Imagination, Heart, and Will

THE more gracefully we heed the summary "Thou shalt!" the less grievous will be the inevitable "Thou must!"

The Imagination plays with things earthly. Its serious work is with things unearthly.

Look long enough at dark mysteries and you will shine.

Two errors of low minds: confusing the real with the carnal and the imaginative with the visionary.

Many of the great failures in life redeem life from bankruptcy.

When men ask, Is Life worth living? the sceptical question is oftener prompted by the fatuousness of their pleasures than by the severity of their sorrows.

To deny self is to affirm Selfhood.

"Back to Nature!" It is the cry of angels about to fall!

When men lose the sense of their grandeur they become grandiose, retaining the pose when they have forgotten the part.

"Shut your mouth!" is a coarse command. All the same in the whole of morals there is no precept more sound and worse needed.

For spiritual beings Life is a story which is complete only when it never ends.

To manage learning nobly requires as much moral power as to manage animal passions nobly.

Primitive minds are enslaved to fanciful fictions; sophisticated minds to fashions—which are servile fictions.

Humility is a virtue practised without effort by the lowliest of saints and the very highest of aristocrats.

When the curtain falls we shall see what is behind it. It is the fear of its falling that keeps us blind.

Humility is sanity in excelsis.

The Intellect should be shaken out of its groove of conformities. The Heart should be planted deep in the furrow of its loyalties.

Between a saint and a fanatic there is all the difference that exists between a fervor and a fever, a surrender and a seizure, a soft and beautiful light and the voluptuous fierceness of fire.

Do not be so prosy as to be merely accurate; have imagination enough to be true!

Look within, but look deep! The Intimate which it is hard to know is the key to the Ultimate which you must know.

Hunger unsatisfied is for souls. Give to beasts the unbearable curse of Satiety!

We have come upon an age of literary habits in which pen is synonymous with sty.

There is no wider gulf dividing men, none across which it is more difficult to throw intercommunicating speech than that which separates the sensitive from the gross, the fine from the coarse.

There is a true second childhood. It consists in making the happier dreams of Long Ago substantial with the reality of Ever-and-Ever.

Old dogs are quite willing to be taught new tricks—provided the new are just like the old.

Defiance is a good club but a poor staff.

Thought and experience are the great enemies of eloquence. They are however the moving energies and living soul of Persuasion.

Words may carry Thought; they break down when they try to carry Feeling.

One disease it is almost impossible to cure—Vulgarity. When complicated with learning it is never cured.

Spontaneous laughter is too near to ecstasy to be possible to that coroner who sits on the corpse of Joy—the Pedant.

There are Monarchs of Mind and Sovereigns of Spirit. But of the flesh there are only saturnalian Clown-kings, flat-faced Khans, and slobbery Sultans.

In a rich life there are three periods, Play, Work, and Thought. The last phase is the most fortunate, for Play has contributed to it the imagination which lightens, and Work the disillusion which darkens.

Do not look for Perfection. But by all means expect it.

To forgive is to blind ourselves to our own wound in order not to see the deformity of the person who inflicted it.

Sexual passion is the greatest of all examples of how an inferior capacity overcompensates itself for its inferiority by blustering its way to arrogant usurpation.

What Death will lay low let not Life set up too high.

The most glorious deeds are done without glory.

Speech is for commonplace transactions. When we are stirred to the soul's depths we are inarticulate. If only we *saw,* should we ever speak, or anyhow ever speak prose?

Bergson is right. In the pursuit of pleasure we have annihilated joy.

When after many studious years we have buried quantities of scientific and philosophic theories, systems of thought, and delusions of erudition, who can blame us for turning to the imperishable divinations of heart and imagination for the sight of something that is not a galvanized corpse?

Res severa gaudium, says Seneca. It is a stern heart that Joy chooses for her dearest dwelling.

Many an arctic soul moves us to pity because its fossil flora indicates that once it was fertile and lived under a benignant sky.

Certain of the censors who blame us for being anthropomorphic in religion have no objection to our being theriomorphic in morals.

When discouraged Intellect surrenders it is frightened Imagination that hauls down the flag.

You will promote your peace and lessen your pain if you bestow your beneficences generously, but as though no such thing as gratitude existed.

The irreverent are poisonous even when they laugh.

When our most august visitors, Beauty for example, and Honor and Faith, knock at the door of our shabby house they come to call for us, not upon us.

The world is with us but we are elsewhere.

The universe sings; else there would be no poets.

One great difficulty in reformers is that they are so fevered for a programme that they forget the pattern.

Morality must sometimes deal severely with a coddled conscience.

Imagination is stimulated only by an object which is distant from the eye; but it has to be very near the heart.

It is better to live under the shadow of death than to die of the gift of life.

Looking into darkness will correct the optical illusions produced by staring at too brilliant a light.

Eels live in the shallow waters of rivers as long as they are immature. For the process of propagation they migrate from the shallows and return to the abysses of the sea, their first home and their last. Peppery advocates of grand causes and new religions, make note of it!

There are permitted trees that bear forbidden fruit.

When a man writes his wrongs he adopts one of the poorest ways of righting them.

Be voluble on the harm of resisting impulses! Be silent on the disaster of violating principles! Haven't you heard of pedagogical and psychological theories based on this beautiful doctrine?

You would convert a person of barbarous manners to considerateness and decency? Give yourself half a chance! Wait till he dies and begin with his grandson!

Love, the madcap, indeed exaggerates. But he is a deep logician. He knows that in the grand concerns of life and happiness you have to falsify the premises in order to arrive at the right conclusion.

Love is eloquent but incurious. It makes its affirmations too soon and asks its questions too late.

To love by self-giving is the rapture of Love. To love by self-withholding may be its majestic sceptre and royal crown.

Love as a precept and obligation roams the earth exchanging chilly salutations with tens of thousands. Love as spontaneous human joy lives in a small house with space for only two. Love as mystical and wholly heavenly requires an entire universe which yet has room for only One.

To remember is to embellish or to embitter.

Love is naturally an honest and decent imp. But a long and sad experience with counterfeits and counterfeiters has overborne his scruple at giving to brass the polish of gold.

The sword-wielding angels on guard at the gates of Love's Lost Paradise admit the innocents who have never yet dwelt there but slay the forlorn of memory who seek to reënter.

The back of Love is broken by the absence of burdens.

Despair results oftener from the absence of Love than from the departure of Hope.

In these days most likely the immortal pair should be called Cupid and Psychosis.

Hope is the richer because Time has disinherited it.

"*N'importe,* it doesn't make any difference!" may be the word either of sunken despair or of soaring hope; of despair if it means that the Worst is bound to win; of hope if it means that the Best can never lose.

Existence cannot perfect the mind if it wrecks the heart. Non-fulfilment of heart is non-sense to mind.

It is a mistake to offer to our love too big and too diffuse an object. We cannot love a universe or a spiral nebula or a solar system. We can only gape at them. We cannot love an empire unless it is symbolized by one emblem created and sustained by Imagination. We cannot love forty-eight states unless by the white magic of exorcising fancy we cancel their several "sovereignties." It is doubtful whether we can love humanity although sentimentality is ready to lift commiseration and sympathy into the usurped seat of Love. But give us the one face, the "raptured touch of the destined hand," the single heart that vitalizes ours, and all the seven seas of Love move their mighty tides to that small and sacred island-shore. We love all persons by first genuinely loving one.

In a soldier of life as in a soldier of war, private discontent with orders given and tasks allotted is inevitable, but open mutiny unpardonable.

As we grow top-heavy with intellectuality our old imp-playmate Fancy pines away from neglect. Too bad! He would have kept us close to roses, thrushes, humming-birds, whispering woods, lisping brooks, and other miraculous and ageless things; would have tickled us by pointing out the funny side of pedantry and pedants; and perhaps would have made us nimble-witted enough to see something of humbug in the pompous port of death.

The eye of calculation is fixed on the main chance; the eye of conscience on the main crisis.

Loving is the heart's journey; Love is the journey's end.

"I will give," is the nectar that vitalizes Love; "I will forgive," the heavenly medicine that restores him when stricken; but "I demand," is the poison that kills him.

When experience disillusions, the antidote for the poison is not more experience but a capacity for higher illusion.

Self-completion *with* others constitutes geniality and sociableness. Self-completion *through* others is a subordinate form of superiority. Self-completion *in* others is the profound principle of both wisdom and love.

When lost Love has been found and returned by Pity it is usually in a damaged condition. When found and returned by Gratitude it is more beautiful than ever.

Life's richest generosity in loving may spring from the nutrient dust of perished love.

A man may be called upon to die for people that he could not possibly live with.

Hope has a twin brother named Despair, who knows history and has reconciled himself to the status quo ante.

The priceless white rose of love is heavily armored with thorns. Anyone may look at it or covet it, but only those who shrink not from laceration may pluck it and wear it.

Man's fundamental need is for ecstasy.

The very greatest souls soar while all unconscious of having wings.

It is because the Sensualist is bankrupt that he leaves nothing to Imagination.

Truth sometimes has to add an inch or two of artificial height to its stature in order to march shoulder to shoulder with Charity.

The dying of a soul is usually more protracted and more appalling than dissolution of the body. It is the only kind of dying that is worth one moment of a wise man's attention.

Every step upward in human existence marks an advance from a disposition to loud laughter to a capacity for deep and secret joy.

Loftiness is Loneliness.

Love is the touchiest of orthodoxies and the most drastic of dictatorships. Its saints are its slaves.

Of all the periods of human life youth is the worst; of all the qualities of human nature youthfulness is the best.

Love is not an "affair" of the heart. It is the heart's consuming business, its whole cycle of peril and peace, its statesmanship and warfare, its commonwealth and kingdom, its ever-and-ever, its election, redemption, and salvation.

We are too inclined to look upon the heavenly side of enthusiasm and the earthly side of the enthusiast.

Think from time to time not of the little that you own, but of the immensity that you owe.

Suppose that in the course of evolution a race of animals that had acquired a new and higher variation, i.e., perfection, distrusted it, refused to use it, and kept reverting to its condition before the perfection arrived. Degeneracy, or at least stagnation, would be the inevitable result. But brutes never commit so manifest a piece of foolishness; they leave that to man!

Ventriloquism—or belly-speaking—has become one of the accomplishments of psychology and philosophy. Apocalypse—or revelation-speaking—has become one of the antiques of religion.

The metal of man's soul was made to ring, not to whine.

The two chief roads to unhappiness and inner destitution are Ego and Nego.

The terrible havoc of sin is that it intensifies individuality and disintegrates personality.

When a man adds to his money, his pleasure, or his knowledge, he simply has something More. When he wins an achievement of the spirit he has something Else.

Love speaks a language in which there is no "If," or else nothing but "If." Both its rapture of assurance and its anguish of doubt are absolute.

From the grapes of Happiness what wine of Sorrow can be pressed!

When we have dissected the intuitive we have lost its energy and inspiration.

To a heart that has suffered long starvation it is dangerous to offer the rich food of love.

It is ages that are transient; it is moments that are everlasting.

One of the greatest crises of life arises when a reflective and contemplative person who delights in cultivating ideal thought is brusquely ordered by harsh conscience to make a decision for ideal action.

The worst of our griefs are too dark and too dense to inflict anything so passionate as a pang. And the highest of our joys are too innocent and too pure to produce anything so voluptuous as a pleasure.

Genuine humility does not arise from the sense of our pitiable kinship with the dust that is unworthy of us but from the realization of our awful nearness to a magnificence of which we are unworthy.

Per aspera ad astra! from footpath to orbit, from cage to constellation, from fetters to firmament, from fever to incandescence, from gleam to glory!

We enrich the world by the insight which shows how poor it is.

Young Love attributes perfection to the Beloved. Waning Love demands it.

You may imitate fervor successfully so long as nobody tries to warm his heart at the imitation.

Love hits many a shrewd and piercing blow, but his stroke is fatal to only one victim—Death.

Life and Death alike are shadows: Life the less noticed because closer to the Night, Death the definitely darker because nearer to the Light.

The universe tempts men to precipitate theories. History seduces them to antiquated experiments. Tradition beguiles them to impossible loyalties. Flux and disillusion everywhere—in arrogant schools, lofty institutions, imposing creeds! Let two or three of us therefore seek fellowship with the contemplative. With them or nowhere can we find the golden satisfactions which should be the richest gift of Time, and the Tranquillity of assurance which is the sacramental sign of Truth.

Stop surrendering to Time like a mercenary! Throw yourself upon it like a conqueror! Close your ears to the whine that now sets the tune of learned decadence! If you cannot find any of the erudite to tell you how to meet life—as you probably cannot—go to the peasant at his plough. In him you will see a wholesome man accepting life and labor, love and joy, pain and death, simply and bravely and without degenerate declamation. Do likewise, and you have done a true man's work. The remaking of the world leave to the lords of foolscap; it is their windy trade! And with equal promptitude of soul throw yourself upon Eternity, fearless and expectant! Eternity too is under the dominion of Character and can but unroll to full consummation the vision, the fortitude, and the sincerity of Spirit, that high Sovereign by Whose law all existence maintains its order and marches onward into Light.

Without a covering of courtesy, charity, and reverence nothing is more repulsive than the naked Truth.

Between the promises of Passion and the prophecies of Spirit choose we must. Passion insists upon choosing for us. Spirit offers to choose with us.

The least significant question that could be asked concerning an earthly life is how long it lasts; the most significant, how long the realities that it serves, trusts, and loves deserve to last.

Despair knows what it has lost. Hope dares not guess what it expects to win.

Our backs grow strong from repeated burdens but break from a single blow.

Intellect masters Nature. But the subjugated jade is disloyal to her sovereign. For when Intellect locks up his runaway relative, Imagination, in the oubliette of dungeon-Fact, Nature throws in through a crack in the ceiling a sight of the stars, a swish of the sea, a gleam of azaleas, the fragrance of roses, the golden bubbling of the thrush, and a whisper of the talk of lovers walking in the light of the moon. Intellect can do nothing then but appeal to the synod of pedants to have his raving step-brother certified as an incurable lunatic.

Love must give his crown into the keeping of Fidelity if it is not to be snatched away by the unscrupulous usurper, Disillusion.

Grief is a visitation; Time will efface it. Joy is a seizure; the next sundown will obliterate it. But Love is an absolute possession; its dominion is timeless; its name is Forever.

Often the tendency to jump to conclusions comes less from restless feet than from aching wings.

With so crumbling a crust for the feet of Life to stand on, it is a wonder that there is so much happiness. With so profound a peace six feet down it is a wonder that there is so much sorrow.

No man is wholly lost till he degrades what he tries to love.

Imagination has been worked too hard in the service of Love and not hard enough in the service of Truth.

The unpardonable sin? The commonest one of all—heartlessness!

The metal of a stout soul rings when struck. The chords of a weak one whine when a breeze blows.

Corruption does not smell so bad in poetry as in philosophy. For in the errant poet we are indulgent to the demonic excess of abnormal sensitiveness and explosive emotion. The profligate philosopher, however, has not the excuse of sudden seizure and momentary mania. He is a studious artificer of the debased, the practised calculator of the gross. What was demonic in the poet becomes demoniac in him. While the poet was obsessed he is possessed. Where the poet was romantic he is necromantic. Where the poet rushes after art into the dark he practises the black art as a settled inhabitant of the pit. What William James once said of the theories of a Harvard colleague: "It is the perfection of rottenness in a philosophy!" was true enough of the man against whom the reproach was directed; but no similar charge could properly be brought against any poet that ever lived.

Mercy means judging human nature by its needs, not its deeds.

Nobody who has been inoculated with moral indignation will ever contract the unclean disease of hate.

Satire is an assault delivered upon humbug and hypocrisy by maddened morality. It is possible only in an age which has fallen but is not yet impenitent.

If only the arrogance of the flesh produced in us the disgust we feel at the arrogance of the fleshly!

It is a corrupt education that makes us magnify what we have and despise or disfigure what we are.

Whither is more important than Where, and Whence matters not at all.

The souls that see and do not argue will still convince when all the dialecticians are dust.

If you are collecting strange examples of stupefying superstition, go much farther than the tribal lore of savages and the folk-tales of peasants. Don't overlook pedagogy and psychology, the genealogical tables constructed by the fortune-telling type of evolutionist, and the rosy romanticists who tell you that Bolshevik Russia is no longer interested in promoting revolution in other countries.

Of all the frozen phrases the term "ethical system" is the most completely refrigerated. If morality means applying human energies to righteousness the first concern of ethics should be to quicken those energies, to lift, illuminate, and inspire them—that is, to put into the moral endeavor passion, loyalty, and love. But what ethical system ever yet raised the temperature of Love by a fraction of a degree? One Teacher there was who put the wings of rapture upon the soul in search of Right, but he never called his teaching a system nor congealed it into the frore formulas of ethics.

Our sharpness of apprehension is revealed not in what we see but in what we divine. Not by eyesight but by awareness, not by observation of outlines but by sensitiveness to atmospheres, not by Touch but by Tact do we penetrate to the essence of reality. This delicacy in piercing through gross Figure to subtle Form and animating Soul is the original, unmistakable, and perpetual mark of genius. To remain in the lumpish and to construct a discourse, a dialectic, and a philosophy of obtrusive bulk, of measurable mass, and of clamorous actuality is the tribal tattooing of the mediocre.

The theatrical persons who call themselves neo-pagans have, they say, lost all illusions. They have not. They retain the stupendous illusion that they are pagans. But it is impossible to observe in them the beauty, the wisdom, the patriotism, the happiness, the devoutness, the magnificent mythology that characterized paganism. And if these neo-pagans are angry at what a Paul Elmer More or an Irving Babbitt or a Chesterton says of them, what would be their anguish at hearing what authentic paleo-pagans would say of them—an Aeschylus for example, or a Virgil, a Seneca, a Pindar, a Plutarch, Plato, or Cicero? It would be a rude Doric or a robust rustic Latinity indeed, we may be sure, in which these veritable sons of paganism would reject the upstart claim to consanguinity. Paganism is a word too stately to be coveted as an illiterate nickname. Those that presume to adopt it should be something more than plagiarists and body-snatchers.

Strong characters fight desperately against Time and Death. It is often their only weakness.

Man is afraid of dying. But that is nothing compared to his dread of being reborn.

From a teacher of the very greatest mind we come away saying: "What a great heart!"

The people who get the least out of life are those whose first principle it is to get the most out of it.

We would rather that our wishes should *come* true than that they should *be* true.

Man the inexhaustible subject exhausted in the exhaustible object—that is Pessimism.

How shall we define man? Judged by his less serious faults of temper and disposition he is an enormous baby, joining the unconscious selfishness of the cradle to the deliberate perverseness of maturity. Judged by his worst wickedness he is the filthiest and cruelest animal that defiles the earth. Judged by his unobtrusive decencies and never-failing heroisms he is a thing that makes beautiful the frame of Nature that houses him. Judged by his possibilities, which now and then are actualized in supreme souls, he is an apparition half reminiscence and half prophecy, unexplained and unexplainable by his natural history or historical evolution, a glorious being for whom no destiny that is not divine is adequate. Let us define him then as a creature capable of creating hell with all its senseless havoc or heaven with all its splendid and heroic beauty, but incapable of averting the doom or missing the fulfilment consequent upon his choice of the havoc or the beauty.

The progress of human character consists in advancing from the somnolent safety of an irresponsible human animal to the incessant peril of a moral person.

One form of the fall of man consists in descending from a Now-and-Ever to a Now-or-Never.

Never confuse Purity with Purism. The former is virtue, the latter virtuosity.

The struggle for worthy existence is won by those who refuse to spend their strength in the struggle for mere existence.

Loyalty is so fierce and contagious an energy that it is safe only when the object of it is something that we can love or worship when we are alone.

We reach the solid substance of enduring Personality by casting off the clinging and smearing accidents of transient individuality.

The Intellect may be a backward pupil in the school of Taste.

Facts become false when Imagination plays *with* them; but they become true only when Imagination plays *upon* them.

Bare fact may be naked nonsense. The exact quantity of beans consumed in Boston in 1888; the precise number of bow-legged carpenters in Czecho-Slovakia or of white roosters in Peru; the census-figures of bullfrogs in Zanzibar; and the Siamese word for gargling the throat—all these are facts, deadly, exact, and paralyzing facts. But what earthly good are they, and wouldn't it be justifiable homicide to lay low a man who should try to unload them upon us?

On the other hand King Lear is not a fact, nor is Hamlet, nor Portia, nor Galahad, nor Pompilia. Every line written about them, judged by bare fact, is false. Yet they are immortally true and imperishably beautiful, and any one of them is worth all the fact-dumps on earth. A fact has to be assumed or subsumed into something other than fact; it must have a value for reason and a set of connections in a rational universe or it is alienated from meaning and becomes non-pertinent and useless. And a fiction that has this meaning and so reveals that Something-beyond-Fact is true. For Truth belongs not to the enumeration and measurement of dead objectivity but to life and understanding. It is an instrument of insight into a cosmos of Spirit. The mark of Truth is to be apocalyptic, to reveal something behind appearance. Therefore it is that we possess not only the sense-perception which would give us dead facts but reason and imagination, the one essential work of which is to apprehend the life-in-fact, the more-than-fact, the world-rationality that gives interest and significance to fact. If fact is sacred it is not its brute anatomy that declares it, but the halo round its head.

We are beasts and angels. And among the angels the most seraphic Presence is the beast that has been tamed and redeemed.

The pessimist argues that life is insignificant because death inevitably overhangs it. The seer declares that death is insignificant because life invincibly overtakes it.

Disillusions of the mind hurt less than disillusions of the heart, but they inflict a deeper wound and are more likely to leave us crippled for life.

Light, says the new physics, has weight; but what presses anguish from the heart is Darkness, which has none.

The Promised Land of Spirit is offered jointly to head and heart. While they fiercely dispute for the larger share, the Philistines of sense who care nothing for light and have not so much as heard of the Holy Spirit of Love, march in, take possession, and lay waste.

With the fading of Love's rose of ecstasy the thorns grow sharper.

When Love breaks a heart it leaves a lingering light that shines wondrously but keeps the wound from healing.

Memory is the point of the sword that pierces us with the pang of beatitude.

Psychic conflicts are very bad. They do us a mischief and make us crazy, say the learned. But why so? We are constituted and equipped precisely for psychic conflicts, and if we had sense enough to use the equipment they would be no different from all our other conflicts, theoretical and practical, from refuting an argument to getting a job. The possession of a will, ideals, loyalties, conscience, and religion is an indication of our preparation in armament and armor for psychic conflicts and for winning a victory in them. Psychic conflict is not a disease; it is the essential condition of our being any good at all. Psychic conflict, the severest possible, was undergone by all righteous rebels who took arms against their tyrant-kings. This Republic is founded upon a stupendous psychic conflict. Yet Hampden and Milton and Cromwell and Washington incurred no disease from the conflict, and, thank Heaven, never consulted a psychiatrist. Luther and Savonarola and Wiclif and Paul—yes, and Jesus—tore themselves loose from tradition, from inherited church, from beloved associations, in appalling psychic conflict; and if they were disordered as a result of it, let us pray to be similarly infected. Psychic conflict is the parent-source of character. If to-day it is producing the defeated, the incapacitated, and the insane in numbers that terrify us for the future of the race, it is because we are destroying the soldierly spirit, pampering souls with falsehood, deriding heroic ideals, vilifying valorous example, stimulating selfishness, discountenancing sacrifice, and emptying existence of radiance and heroism and trust and hope.

Love at last grows hungry on the food of rapture. It is kept from starvation by the homely fare of Common Sense.

Everything is illusion except the soul which can understand, suffer, and survive disillusion.

The highest stage of Reason is not knowledge but Illumination.

The most important question for any man, whether he is thinker, student, college president or day laborer, is not what science or philosophy presents to him as plausible or proved, but whether he shall confront experience and interpret life with a delicate, chivalrous, and high-toned spirit or with common, vulgar, and blackguard mind.

It is unfamiliarity that breeds contempt just as it is darkness that breeds things that crawl.

The more majestic the orbit the vaster the traversed emptiness; the more brilliant the star the darker the night!

Our souls do not earn much on earth. We live on an endowment.

To men as to vultures great heights offer advantages for spying out carrion.

It is useful to remember that hell as well as heaven has its mighty fervors, its intense energies, its tremendous will, its devoted legions, its prodigious throne!

An epigram is a bee that may sting in its search for nectar.

There is one suffering too awful even for hell—to endure penalty without seeing the sublimity of its justice.

"Knowledge is power!" and the maxim is never completed. The missing words are: "for good or for evil."

We might be contented with the sty were it not for the awful memory of what we took into it.

The kind of inner world that we live in determines the quality of the thoughts and purposes that we live with.

The chord underwent the stretched torment of the vise before it was fit to sing.

If sense-perception exaggerated, it would falsify the picture of the world. Unless imagination exaggerated it would falsify the meaning of the world.

The first faculty that the decadent loses is the sense of smell.

Men of austere principles should send their principles out into the world but keep the austerity at home.

Men are trying to give up heroic hope. But they are miserable from the recognition that if they give it up they cease to be heroic.

Thought, purpose, logic, industriousness, but without radiance or love: Isn't it an accurate description of Satan?

Caiaphas was likely enough a good neighbor, kind to children, and perhaps generous to the poor. And Torquemada probably liked to hold little lads on his knee. Yet they were murderers both! The signpost of the minor virtues is nailed up along the entire route to Hades.

The end of time is not very far from the end of our noses.

Life is a battle in which we fall from the wounds we receive in running away.

Caution is often a genteel term for opaqueness of vision; and courage a complimentary term for boisterousness of bluster.

Love is a devil's advocate who protests against the canonization of Thought.

It is our misfortune that we look at Life with the light of Imagination, but at Death with the darkness of Sense.

Love heals the wounds of Wisdom.

We hunger for Vision and have nothing to eat but Knowledge.

The thinker who descends into the abysses of existence will find himself in a realm impenetrably dark unless, like certain fishes of the far ocean depths, he carries with him his own self-engendered light.

The authentic utterance and native speech of the soul is, could we only hear it: "Surrender to death? Never! I will not surrender even to Frivolity!"

A zealot is a man who would cast swine before pearls.

The Beautiful is not the Good, but grows sickly if torn away from it. And the Good is not the Beautiful, but becomes terrifying without it.

A breaking heart often mends a broken will.

The Pharisee was a good man who became reprobate by patronizing Goodness.

It is extraordinary that we feel no filial piety to Father Ape. He stands, they say, at the head of our line; he achieved the most momentous step ever taken in the history of life; we owe him a debt which it would seem the blackest ingratitude to ignore. Yet no one has ever written ode or anthem to him; nor composed a sonata or overture of pithecoid patriotism to him; nor even put up the cold tribute of a statue to him. He is as remote from our love as our electrons or our chromosomes. Our default in remembrance, however, is not after all absolute. The moral outlook of a lot of our fiction and a good deal of our psychology and philosophy distinctly recalls him. On the other hand this may be only the first indication in zoölogical history of the depravity of the younger and smarter generation.

A discourse made up of abstract ideas is like a breeze blowing through zither-strings—cadence without melody, sweet noises but no tune!

What a barbarous prejudice of Philistines it is that art, literature, and religion are less trustworthy revealers of reality than science or philosophy! or that intuitive insight is more subject to aberration than the academic theories which are always being revoked and the slippery manoeuvres of ratiocination which are forever being found fallacious!

Love bullies Imagination into telling lies. Faith dares it to tell the truth.

It is dangerous to be emotionally infatuated with Truth and Honor. There is only one sound and safe service of these ideals—prompt and harsh obedience.

At the end of Life's long journey old Experience yearns with unavailing sighs for the sight of his childhood Sweetheart, Innocence.

If you have a sense of direction count it not an affliction to be destitute of the sense of locality.

A woman who knows not self-abnegation should marry as fellow-monster a man who knows not self-assertion.

The home in which man dwells longest—the Nursery!

It is terrible when men know that there is within them an ineffable speech of glory, but see nothing and believe in nothing to which they can apply it.

If we must give an account of every idle word, think what a festival the Day of Judgment will be for the spouters who will step forward to give the account!

Man's fighting instinct is a priceless possession. Let it serve priceless causes—and not be wasted in jaw-squabbling round the parish pump or nose-thumbing at a politician's biscuit party!

Malignant wit is a corrosive acid by which low people eat their way out of the cocoon of the commonplace.

Speaking with tongues—the gift of the unholy spirit!

A wise man always, but a fool never, recognizes the existence of retribution.

Common calculation will perhaps restrain us from cruelty or deception. But only an aristocratic and soldierly spirit withholds us from the rabble rowdyism of sensuality.

If your daydreams are such as to serve and flatter you, you are probably a pathological case. If they are such as to summon you bravely and perilously to serve them, you walk in light and with light are filled.

The clever criminal is a person who is unable to grasp moral principles but thoroughly competent to draw practical conclusions from corrupt theories.

The wrong we actually do only inflicts a defeat upon us. The right we even wish to do demands unconditional surrender.

To-day men who are as unreal as Chimaeras are telling us how to be Realists.

When the Heart embraces love, and the Imagination, sublimity, they push prurient Thought as far as possible from the scene.

Don't drop your H's. Do drop your I's.

People see Happiness as they see a ghost. They dare not say it may not be an hallucination, but are quite sure that if the apparition is real that it comes from a higher world.

Love destroys all scruples unless it is willing to accept every sacrifice.

Truth never wears a look so distressed as when her friends clothe her in the grotesque vesture of their prejudices.

On her earnest lovers Truth places her hands in benediction—one hand is Humility which she lays upon their hearts; the other is Mystery which she places upon their heads.

If a man would make himself absolutely incapable of understanding humanity, let him look at human experience with only the staring eye of sterile intellect.

Because of morosely reckoning the reward of a great vocation we may forfeit the priceless bestowal of its pain.

How can we tell that love is genuine, deep, and true? By observing whether it turns aside from calmorous satisfaction to catch the breath of silent sacrifice.

Giving to a wail or a whine the name of cosmic despair confers upon it a grand title but no grandeur.

Power forgets that it is a debtor; Passion, that it is a servant.

Love gives only the ashes of its decay to Thought; the flame of its ecstasy Thought cannot even see.

In the study of history and its great personalities where the chronicler ends the interpreter begins.

Intellect discovers because Spirit divines.

"There was silence in heaven for half an hour!" Too great a strain for uncontrollable demonic gabble! And so perhaps it was that, rebels to reticence and rattling with drivel, Lucifer and his angels fell.

Oratory is a seductive art that may make us forget so important a thing as substance. Preaching should be an awakening revelation that makes us forget so trivial a thing as art.

Our carnal-minded writers are solicitous that their books should contain not atmosphere but effluvia.

Totality is the ideal of all thought. Particularity is the domain of all passion.

The mirror in which Love looks at itself reflects the face of Immortality.

The mind must put on wings even to state a fact about a worm.

We are sunk in a sea of mystery. But what would suffocate us is the absence of mystery.

Frightened assent is worse than ignorant assent. The latter is frequently serious, the former is always servile.

The search of Reason is to find itself and cannot possibly be anything else. But because the search must be meritorious and fit for moral persons the way is beset with tangled irrationality that calls for valor as well as vigilance.

Progress to unknown accomplishments is exciting. But more healthy and not less exhilarating is progress in a known Perfection.

You have classes for teaching style? Very good. But what style is to convey, the swing of its march, the streaming of its banners, the passion of its attack—do not dissect and scholasticize these predestinate potencies till you have taught the oriole by geometry how to build its nest or a bee by chemistry how to change nectar into honey!

Hope is the noblest form of Defiance.

The Moralist frowns and trembles. The Lover laughs and sighs. But it is the Lover after all who has the acuter scruple and the deeper fear.

Love will work his fingers thin in loyal service under poverty, hardship, defeat, or even defamation. But however ample the wages offered him he goes on strike at once against self-idolatrous Egotism.

Surely God will be merciful to us, for we have to bear the humiliations of life and endure the profanation of death.

The free man is a moral being who has found his sure authority and bound himself to its true obedience.

In trying to win the regard of decent people the inquisitive and prying person loses by a nose.

Old Dr. Browne of the *Religio Medici* writes a good Latinized prescription for a tranquil mind: "Be carefully solicitous, not anxiously solicitudinous."

Husbands and wives often so exhaust themselves in building the hive that they have no energy left for visiting the flowers and storing the honey.

A wise man's thought should dwell in a softened twilight composed of imaginativeness still smiling and experience no longer snarling.

Middle age is a zone of silence. When we move on toward the end of the cave, the echoes of youth are heard again.

The feeling of being old may arise not from the length of our lingering but from the delay in our arriving.

The softened light of old age is the merging of two kindred radiances—the lingering glow of the far-off morning and the deep flush of the nearing sunset.

Old age sees the rich fruits of autumn ripen but lacks the will to harvest them, knowing that the coming winter will be otherwise provided for.

The aging are accused of lack of sympathy with youth, whereas it is usually the most pronounced sympathy that they feel. But they have seen through and lived through most of the brilliant discoveries which youth is confident it has made for the first time ever.

Old age should expend its vigor in repairing what has been wasted by the weakness of youth.

If we lived intensely we should die almost surreptitiously.

The wise man turns aside from seeing in order that he may strengthen his vision.

Despair points to the very pit with the finger of Hope.

The learned corrupters of our English speech are holding us to barbarism as with iron bands. To braying dons it chiefly is that we owe such infamies as "factual," "large contacts," "broad viewpoints," "inferiority complex," incessant "evaluations," everlasting "relationships," and that horror of horrors, "mentality." The growth of our colleges corresponds pretty exactly to the decay of our mother-idiom. Indeed the racy slang of the streets is far nearer to the genius of our native tongue than the clownish usage which has spread from the academy to Congress and the Presidency and settled upon the whole country as a national disgrace. It would be a great advance in decency if no man should be allowed to lecture here in a hall of learning unless it is certain that the language that he speaks is English. But this service to culture would doubtless be regarded as sacrilege to science.

Sin is a good blunt word that should have its meaning extended. It should take in a lot of poses and pretenses now regarded as only amusing, a good many habits considered to be merely unconventional, and a few manifestations of severity and bigotry indulgently held to be pardonable excesses of holy zeal and religious virtue.

When a man has sold his soul to a party or a programme, every act he does is the act of a slave and every other word he utters is a lie.

Do not be forever analyzing water. Sometimes drink it!

If a time comes to you in which by some blazing outburst of light or some overwhelming pressure of creative darkness you come to understand that human speculation is more a fumbling with aimless hands than seeing with clear eyes; that our possession of knowledge is small and our pretense to knowledge enormous and arrogant; that it is vastly more important for you to leave upon mortal circumstance the impress of a soldierly and expectant spirit than to shut yourself up in an ivory tower with fancies, moods, and theories disdainful or sentimental; that creeds are signposts, but set awry; that creedlessness is no less deceptive; but that there are a few mighty souls who have passed by and that your place is beside them; that you are under orders and must redeem life's humiliation and disillusion by fidelity to them; and that the inexhaustible and never to be rationalized or systematized resources of existence justify our highest hopes and give substance and promise to our deepest joy: then you may forget your birthday and begin to celebrate the day of your veritable creation.

Since degeneracy dares not appeal to Honor and abjures Character, it reaches out a grasping hand to the Ideal as a respectable cover for its rottenness.

KING THIEF

The typical figure of our age is not bard nor prophet, not priest nor soldier nor thinker. It is the Thief. Wealth in vast quantity and variety exists in the world, and there is not a more characteristic effort of the time than to steal it, nor a greater display of ingenuity and brazen shamelessness than in devising methods of stealing it. The unscrupulous procession of thieves is led by proud states and lofty statesmen. They wheedle loans from their own and other peoples, never intending to pay them back and regarding it as an affront if their victims ask them back. National legislatures become thieves' accomplices by voting away enormous sums of public money to terrorizing groups organized for plunder. The thief in public office, the thief under the shelter of the law and as an officer of the law, the thief in crooked finance, the thief by highway violence, the thief by petty larceny, the thief as a cozener, pilferer, grafter or Lord Chancellor—there he stands in the forefront of the age, as destitute of conscience as a snake, as absorbent as a sponge, as magical in his touch as Midas, as serene in the prerogatives of his dark domain and as sure of a subservient following as Lucifer. Socialism looks leniently upon the thief. Communism canonizes him. And preachers in plenty are ready to give him a sprinkling of baptismal innocence if he only steals from the right people and in the proper cause. Preachers once sanctified murder provided it was a heretic that was murdered. The successors of these luminaries of ethics now lay their hands in blessing upon the pickpocket if only the pocket-picking is done for the hastening of the Great Society and the Millennial Day.

Nothing can be done about it. The very word "thief" is regarded as impolite, violent, and harsh if applied to respectable scoundrels or to leaders of noble reform. But to be bound by obligation, to bear the burden of honor, to be sensitive to moral debt and responsibility, to postpone our own advantage till we have quitted ourselves of what we owe to others—are all becoming foreign and soon perhaps will be fantastic notions. The thief gives promise of winning a recognized, as he now has an unacknowledged, prestige and power. Our only hope is that when all honest men have been robbed, thieves will be so industrious in stealing from one another that for very safety's sake they will begin to observe the sixth commandment, not as a precept of divine law but as a counsel of profitable prudence.

3. Reflection and Philosophy

Die Theile habt Ihr in eurer Hand
Nur leide fehlt das geistige Band.
GOETHE

"Existence its pieces upon you has hurled;
Till Spirit unites them they're Chaos, not World."

THE worst delusion of our age is that men are trying to construct a psychology of life upon a metaphysic of death.

Materiality is no more the meaning of the universe than sensuality is the meaning of man.

The most stupendous sort of nonsense it is impossible to utter unless one is very learned.

Disillusion may become the most petted and fondled of all illusions.

Illusion is the name that we often give to a truth of which we are not worthy.

It is all very well to push scientific inquiry into the most minute details that we can reach; but we may remember that an X-ray photograph is an abominably poor likeness.

Science means seeing fragments of the universe with a fragment of the mind.

If we are looking for an example of fatuous wish-thinking we may consider the men who are trying to make our small bit of the universe glorious and all the rest of it contemptible.

The foundation of science is the supremacy of the rational. The foundation of Religion is similar but deeper—the perpetuity and victoriousness of the rational.

Hardly a single scientific certainty of the nineteenth century is left standing. But not one of the heroic souls and seers of fifty years ago or thirty centuries ago is antiquated or eclipsed. The course of Knowledge is marked by tombstones; the course of Faith by emptied tombs.

We begin our study of philosophy hopefully asking "What am I?" Likely enough we are soon wailing "Where am I?" And in our final prostration we may even come to the dying gasp: "What! Am I?"

Space-Time, Body-Mind, Ideal-Real, Flesh-Spirit, Appetite-Aspiration—all mismated marriages, each of the partners speaking a language not understood by the other, forever clashing, and forever threatening divorce, yet hanging together for the sake of the children, who are the Universe, Life, Experience, and Character!

From the debris of Intuition we build a patchwork of myth—the universe of science.

What makes a rational world? The capacity of objectivity to answer and fulfil subjectivity—the response of inexhaustible fullness to an illimitable need of being filled.

Science explores the universe that is presented to us: Religion, the universe that is represented in us.

Scientific explanation simply adds one mystery more to the mysteries that are "explained."

The scattered letter-blocks of existence, if they are to be made intelligible at all, must be set in an order that spells Purpose, the primary mark of intelligibility.

Since in Philosophy there is so much smoke, in Religion there must be some fire.

Life is a sea of clouded horizons and unfathomable depths, of hurricane storms and halcyon calms. It sweeps on to inaccessible shores. It moves its mighty tides in answer to mysterious forces acting from the firmament on high. Its moods are incalculable, its energies too stupendous for reckoning, its dark foundations hidden in a silence impenetrable and everlasting. In its presence we may wonder, we may hope, we may worship—and all these attitudes are reasonable if not inevitable. But one thing we may not do. We may not take Rationalism's pint pot, marked off in exact gradations, and with the roar of those mighty waters in our ears, boast that the ridiculous vessel suffices to hold the emptied abyss.

The metaphysical search can be satisfied only by a spiritual discovery.

The vocation of philosophy is to attempt the magnificent arduousness of the commonplace.

There is a spicy flavor to negation. But negation is very stale fish if offered as either explanation or fulfilment.

Thought seeks the shadows knowing that Light cannot be far off.

If an argument only supports our opinions we care little whether it is too weak to support itself.

A solved problem only raises another unanswerable question which in turn calls for one more unintelligible solution.

Inference is Intuition cautiously extended. Intuition is Inference audaciously anticipated.

The streak of vulgarity appears in unexpected places. There are to-day philosophers and psychologists who seem to be boasting that they have the dirtiest cots in the lazaretto of learning.

Mind has a floor but no roof, a starting-point but no stopping-place.

There are two types of thought—the Hither and the Hither-Yonder. The more the Hither type analyzes itself intellectually, the nearer it approaches to the Yonder. And the more the Hither-Yonder type experiences itself spiritually, the further it recedes from the Hither.

The logician's vexation comes from realizing by how narrow a margin an argument misses Truth. The thinker's melancholy arises from perceiving by how immense a distance Thought misses it.

It is the whole which is lost when we ignore the particular.

When Reason speeding toward the rational hits the gross lump of sense-perception the resulting thud is Matter.

When we rationalize a thing we transubstantiate it into something higher than Thinghood.

An open mind that lets everything in should be well provided with exits.

Do not be deluded by the starved abstraction, bare Fact! but miss not a single point of full-featured pure Fact!

The chief good of certain philosophers is that they exasperate other philosophers.

Constance in *King John* utters the easiest of all petitions to answer: "Preach some philosophy to make me mad!"

Pragmatism is a street orchestra that plays the pipes and pounds the drum not for the music but for the collection.

Theories of experience are devised by people who imagine that excogitation can be a substitute for experience.

There is a skeleton in the closet of philosophic Thought—Common Sense.

How few philosophers who are eloquent on the authority of Reason inquire into the reason for the authority!

Philosophic thought is inchoate ecstasy too timid to intensify itself.

Philosophers speak of the world of things as "the Given." Some of them never hear the soul's protest: "Given? I cannot accept it; there must be more!"

A philosopher should be an athlete of thought, not an acrobat of opinion.

We explain mysteries by the greatest of all mysteries—the need for explanation.

There are philosophers who instead of thinking man out think him away and then speculate profoundly upon the insubstantiality of the hole that he has left.

Philosophy is stale because its experts have substituted a technical puzzle and a professional virtuosity for a spiritual and poetic mystery.

The essence of a Thing is that it is an event bounded by Time. The essence of Spirit is that it is an energy bound in Time.

The philosopher's ideal of Pure Thought might perhaps be forwarded to realization by pure thoughts.

Many an error is "proved." The real refutation of it is that you can only talk it but cannot live it.

Thought is an energy that shapes. The soul is an instrument of insight that finds each shape a shade.

Taking too vigorous a bite of tough problems after the milk teeth of Thought's babyhood have dropped out, but before the true teeth meant for adult mastication have grown, is the making of many a wounded pessimist.

One trouble with philosophy is that the method by which it departs from superficial appearances, which do not satisfy, is not the method which will lead it to the underlying reality which does satisfy. Logical criticism is enough for the former. But for the latter there is need for the rarest gift of Heaven—spiritual penetration, comprehension, elevation, and audacity. A profound philosopher is harder to find than a saint or a poet, for he combines the highest qualities of both.

The philosopher tries to show how little of our "phantasms" of sublimity is objectively real; the poet and the believer, how much of them is subjectively necessary.

A universe is not made by a world of things being given to the mind but by a mind being given to a world of things.

Many an idea had originally a reason for existing but has none at all for going on.

Nothing or zero has an important value in mathematics. But you have to go to philosophy to find a value for Nothingness.

"Let us start with something that we can understand!" The reasoner who says that must be very raw or very youthful.

The strong drink of philosophy should not be taken on an empty heart.

In some loose and poetically scientific sense no doubt there is uniformity in Nature—but *Gott sei Dank!* we need not fear the monotony of it; for Nature is too vital to be uniform for three seconds in succession.

Nature asks us to understand ourselves profoundly once for all, not to keep on explaining her superficially for ever and ever.

There are philosophers who, as they uncover region after region of what they call experience, are able to produce in us thoughts no more significant than the tears we shed in peeling an onion.

The manifold world of things conspires to make one universe. The multiple world of ideas stretches toward one Truth. The varied world of our loves draws toward one Ideal. In all existence inward and outward all additions approach one Sum; all divisions point to an original Unity; all parallels converge at one point; all fragments combine in one Ground; all souls find coherence in one Soul.

Scientists should accept the emancipation of poetry. Poets should refuse subservience to Science.

A paradox that would reward inquiry is that a man of science must be intensely interested in disinterested research.

It is a sophistry to interpret experience in terms of illusion; for the terms that denote the illusion are furnished by experience; and we could not recognize illusion unless we knew an experience that was not illusory.

The belief that reason is supreme is not a product of reasoning. It is an intuitive apprehension of truth so certain that it would be insane to doubt it, so sure that argument would profane it. Life and thought rest upon a foundation of intuitive understanding at last. We have, that is, a capacity for immediate and infallible insight into reality. No man can speak a sentence without presupposing it; no thinker utter a proposition without implying it. What is this instantaneous vision, this wholeness of primary comprehension? What does it mean? Where does it lead? Professional philosophy does little more than ask the question and pass on. Psychology can do nothing but gabble unintelligibly about it. But pure poetry will set your hand upon the door of interpretation and pure religion will swing open the door.

Great convictions produce profound satisfactions. That explains why a good deal of philosophy is artifice and many a philosopher artificial.

Men sprang from apes? But who were these "men" that did the springing?

Knowledge breaks up reality into pieces. But pieces are the surest way to delusion if we forget the Whole which precisely makes them pieces. On these abstractions torn from the total context we build the vast mythology of scientific and philosophical theories. One after another of these doomed conjectures proves misleading and is laid, ever so gently lest scandal arise, in the grave. One day we shall put an end to fortune-telling from the fragments of existence and see the universe of being as a totality, a many-storied manifestation of Power, and Power as something unintelligible except as Will and uninterpretable except as Purpose. Then we shall bear nobly the unloveliness of the lower levels and, recognizing that our very estrangement from them proves them to be unfit for us, make our home on the higher, where all that is partial falls away into the reconciliations of the Principle of the Whole.

When a genius uses artifice the artifice is such as might be envied by reality.

When we see sublimity in Nature the sublimity does not come from Nature. If it did a cat, a toad, a bull, or a bobolink could see it too.

Simplicity is hard, for it is of creation; simplification is easy for it is of manufacture.

Academically we are rated by the content of the head, spiritually by the intent of the will.

If a man has a gift of dramatic and picturesque description, but no taste for reflection, let him confine his historical writing—if write history he must—to descriptions of vivid personalities and romantic episodes. But from discoursing upon institutions, systems of thought, the spiritual principles underlying great religions, and the philosophical ideas interwoven with great cultures, let him withhold the impertinence of his jaunty pen! True, if he persists in the intrusion, he may write a best-seller, but it is his readers who are sold. If you wish an example, there is Mr. Wells's *Outline of History.*

"Thing-in-itself" says the Idealist is an absurdity. The true noumenon and veritable reality is "Thing-in-a-Self."

The infant knocks about his alphabet-blocks unaware that he has in his hands the materials of Shakespeare. The unenlightened pedant knocks about the fragments of existence not knowing that he has in his hands the elements of the discourse of the Eternal.

Psychological erudition is becoming a serious obstacle to psychological insight.

Realism is the effort to disentangle this observable universe from the universe of thought-forms which the mind fetches in on its own account for the representation of this universe. And the rude noise that we hear as the Realist attempts it is the loud laughter of the Idealist.

Scientific method requires that we prosecute our study absolutely free from prepossessions—except of course *this* prepossession.

The Inscrutable is not to be solved; that is the pathos of Mind. But we are inscrutable ourselves; that is the glory of Soul.

Theory leads facts a little further into the light. Faith drags theory a little further out of the dark.

Common sense, the homespun porter at the lodge gate of Intellect, spends much of his burly energy grumbling at the decrepit old tramps and the flashy bounders whom his Master is willing to take in as Guests.

You can perhaps bestow a little wealth upon an impoverished heart; but try not to insert light into a ramshackle head.

To bestow learning on some persons is like sprinkling perfume on a man who never bathes.

Why talk about the decline of faith when learned men believe that an ancient lizard became a winged bird by flapping its forelegs, when millions of people are falling in love and getting married, and when expert psychiatric testimony is accepted in the courts?

The principle of the logician is to plod from premises to a conclusion. The determination of the mystic is to fly to the one Finality which is the premise of all principles and the end of all conclusions.

The true Seeker pursues the Ideal upward. The corrupt teacher hunts it down.

The psychologist, pledged husband of Psyche, is off at present on an adulterous holiday with Aphrodite.

If Nature did not achieve it for us, the digestion of our food or the oxygenation of our blood all the laboratories on earth could not contrive for us. If the acid-alkali balance of the blood or the right proportion of red corpuscles and white had been left to the planning of our brains the human race would have had a very short history indeed. Opulent Nature gives us so much that it is beyond our power to make any return in kind. And Nature desires from us nothing in kind. What she asks is something not in her capacity to possess, the sceptre of thought, the royal robe of beauty, the priceless crown of character. When we explore her physical and physiological processes, she says to us: "Leave these to me!" But of creation of the spirit she implores us: "Give these to me!"

The spirit leaps but logic limps. Try leaping once in a while! The place you land in will most likely justify the venture—and perhaps cure the limp!

The Here-and-Now mind will always be a sick and petulant exile in a Forever-and-Ever universe.

Some savage medicine men have the weird power of hitting their naked bellies with their fists so as to produce quite tremendous sounds. The reverberations furthermore have an occult meaning which is duly interpreted for the awed believers. Those fellows are well on their way to writing novels of the abdominal school or manuals of behaviorist psychology.

Do not smother the soul in the mud of sense. Discover the soul in the seed of sense.

The psychologists who are for the moment in fashion haven't any altar. But if they had one they certainly would feed its fire with dung.

No theory of man can live unless it makes live. A true theory *of* life must be ***unto*** life.

Everything that is logical is teleological.

The perpetual impulse of the soul is to soar. The present habit of its specialists, the psychologists, is to dive.

Matter is thought that has thickened by falling into Time.

The materialist is a man who is intellectually in love with the non-intelligent and the loveless.

If materialism were true, portrait painters and sculptors would require far fewer sittings.

Materialism is impossible because Rapture is irrepressible.

Myth leaves Fact far behind, but never catches up with Truth.

To science Reality is something to be looked into; to religion it is something to be grown into.

Myths are beautiful and profound. It is mythology that is stiff, devitalized, and arid.

The essence of Fact is Fiat.

Common Sense is a delusion if it restricts its perceptions to the common senses.

Truth requires the coöperation of at least two persons, one who is able to speak it, and one who is fit to hear it.

Nothing more brilliantly proves how near we are to Truth than that we know how close we stand to Error.

Love of Truth is not an agonized appetite for more filling. It is a mystical passion for a fulfilling.

The truths of Reality darken the truth in Reality.

Love Truth with a consuming passion? But can anybody rationally do it unless Truth has a consuming passion to return the love?

Mechanism can produce nothing, therefore can fundamentally explain nothing. It is a consequence, not a cause. It is simply the determinate form of an existence predetermined to that form. It is a pattern for things which antecedently require that kind of pattern.

That objectivity is dead and that subjectivity is diseased are the pair of philosophical scullions who produce the illegitimate offspring, Pessimism.

It would be useless to put things together as parts of an artifice called argument unless we saw things together as phases of a finality called Truth.

Any number of clever persons who say that in the universe there is no mind expect the study of that universe to perfect their own minds, and an irrational world to answer their questions rationally.

Zeitgeist is a contradictory word: *Geist* is irreconcilable with *Zeit*.

It is one thing to earn wisdom by study; quite another to accept the alms of wisdom from a study.

When Truth is unable to evoke in us the ardor with which we served Illusion it is not because we think less of Truth but because we regard ardor as a part of the Illusion.

One of our heavy troubles is that a lot of people are confabulating about Truth who know nothing about Life and Experience, Truth's second and third Persons in the indivisible consociation of the divine Abyss.

Truth is seldom desired for its own substantial and sovereign sake. That is why we are so often recommended to seek it but so rarely urged to adore it.

Improbability is the first mark of Truth.

Vituperation retains its insolence everywhere, but as it passes from the fish market to the campus it grows dictionary-dandified. When a man now takes seriously the highest spiritual geniuses of history and seeks a share in their experiences, the bargees of learning call him psychotic and theomaniac. Their biliousness subsides, however, and their vocabulary relapses to drabness in the presence of a beefy Philistine as dull as a codfish and as unimaginative as an earthworm. He, fortunate animal, is simply "normal."

Reality is such that it will answer if you question it. This is the foundation of science. And it will wreck you if you mutilate or ignore it. This is the foundation of morals.

By standing too close to reality we falsify reality. When a painter shows us every pleat in a lace ruffle but cannot show us any light in the eyes of his subject, any vitality in the lips, any character in chin and nose and forehead, he is misrepresenting the reality of a human being. When a novelist morosely concentrates his portraiture of life upon the abdomen of his characters and the impulses that begin and end there he is not a seer but a parodist. If a man should regard a picture of a human face as of less value for realism than an X-ray picture of a man's liver and stomach he would be a perverted monster. Without a more-than-the-real there is no Real. Without the perspective of spirit, without the purification of overlooking, there is nothing that is not hideous, and most hideous of all things is Truth.

Truth is a consequence not so much of propositions that are proved as of perceptions that are purified.

Mere knowledge may be the chief obstacle to Truth.

There is something universal in the mind which can utter the word "Universe."

The Universe without a Soul is a Spectre.

Nothing can have a history which has not a vocation; and a universe which allots vocations must contain fulfilments.

All knowledge of the universe is mind-reading.

To the materialist the universe is a collection of bodies juxtaposed in space. To the spiritual thinker it is an organism of parts coördinated in purpose. The one perceives the *corps,* the other, the *Esprit de corps.*

Isolated Reason disjoined from sympathy, generosity, wisdom, and humor, and hypnotized by the sun-glare of thesis and formula becomes merciless, fanatical, and criminally crazy. By deadly logic it invokes Robespierre's guillotine, Lenin's Cheka, Torquemada's fagots, Philip the Second's prisons, Caiaphas' cross. It creates the saints, who are also the devils, of pedantry.

Kindred to them are the immoralists of our age and of all ages who isolate the physical body and all its impulses from beauty and wonder and tenderness and loyalty—and invoke the hideous Absolute of the flesh as the gracious Lord of incarnate life.

It is not a faith that the earthy pedant seeks primarily to destroy; for him a faith is only a formula, and formulas are his food and drink. What he would dissolve is the rapturous energy and vital zest which a faith confers; for vitality is his poison and abhorrence.

Nothing causes so violent a gnashing of teeth among pedants as the undying supremacy of the geniuses whom the principles of the pedant would have made impossible.

Weak minds hold to dogmas because yesterday's credulity believed them. Minds still weaker reject a faith because to-day's fashion denies it.

A plural uni-verse is a phrase that would have been beyond the audacity of Boyle-Roche himself, the father of bulls.

Our heartiest laughter comes when the irreverent scamp Fancy plays a trick upon brocaded and pontifical Intellect.

We spend immense labor and ingenuity in exploring the whole universe, but even a greater industry and subtlety in refusing to face the whole man.

Perhaps the most wonderful feature of the universe is its "hang-togetherness," and the most significant feature of man is his perpetual search for something to "hang-together" with. Physical things will not do, else there would be no search; nor animal passions, else the search would be a torment, beginning in decay and ending in disaster; nor Humanity, for they are all searching; nor intellectual and artistic cultivation, for it points further on to some Original so partially gained as to make hunger for full discovery more fierce than before. Some there are who have tried Grandeur, even infinite Grandeur; and they send back word that they have found by experience indubitable and triumphant the kinship foreshadowed in estrangement and the communion that crowns coherence.

One delusion of the clever is to fancy that when they sink the universe into a word of two syllables and call it "Nature" they have learned something. And when they sweep the whole system of prodigious processes in the universe into a little phrase of three words—"laws of Nature"—they are fondly sure that they have "explained" something. To some of the learned the dictionary is an adequate substitute for reality.

Between mediaeval clericalism dictating to science and a contemporaneous Sanhedrim of scientific Pedants pontificating upon Religion, the best thing for a plain man to be is a heretic to both impostures.

Intellect, self-satisfied, haughty, and supercilious, is contemptuous toward Feeling with her hungry eyes and toward Imagination with his starry raptures. But it is these two faithful laborers in the factory and mine of experience that furnish the gold and purple with which Intellect adorns his skinny bones.

Intellect will believe anything however shabby—folklore patently nonsensical, dogmas manifestly immoral, scientific conjectures obviously extravagant, psychological aberrations incredible to any mind that is sane. The Intellect is bourgeois and tends to consort with low company. But Heart and Imagination are aristocratic. They refuse to believe in anything that is not magnificent and of stately demeanor, noble voice, and beautiful presence.

A culture can be produced only by a vivifying energy that stirs the soul of a people to great conceptions and to noble forms of beauty fit for the expression of them. A culture is the product of an inward intensity creating congenial outward tone and structure. It is spirit and life giving their superscription to external manifestation. It is an awakening from within, a vital expansion quickened to grace and stateliness and splendor. When therefore we hear pedants declare that they will produce it and make its spontaneous essence a matter of manufacture by eugenics or by psychological witchcraft or behaviorist black magic, we may remember that never yet in the wildest evolutionary dream have flowers grown from granite or flying birds come forth from flying fish.

The mighty Titans were slain for their rebellion by the most high gods. What then shall be the fate of the manikins and miniatures who are imitating the Titanic roar of defiance in falsetto voices behind ginger-colored whiskers?

Mind is meant to conquer things—the soul to conquer Thinghood.

Many theories are entertained by the mind which are refused lodging by the soul.

The more vital, precious, and beautiful a conviction, an ideal, or a belief is, the more deeply beneath the cognitive mind its roots extend.

With the learned Thought is in danger of flying loose from Reality and becoming merely synthetic cerebration.

Turn now and then, O baffled Student, from the windy clamor of the schools and take a walk in the royal road of unlearning.

Among the learned pedagogues there are formidable monitors

who warn us that human nature must not aspire to a Transcendent nor fling its hopes beyond this terrestrial scene. But that is precisely what human nature does and has been doing since it became human! Human nature seems to obey a rule that is different from and more stately than a ferule.

Caught in a clumsy ratiocination, but aching for immediate and intuitive vision—this is what makes us exiles and kings: exiles who await reprieve and kings whose enthroning is postponed.

Learning is sometimes the most easily obtained compensation for inferiority of taste, culture, and character.

Things are enough for Knowledge but not for Knowing.

Scepticism, like many a viper, cannot survive the bite of its own fangs.

Our intelligentsia are forever telling us to acquire "the mature mind." It is a mark of their own immaturity to think that it can be acquired apart from the maturity of something more than mind.

Tired Thinker, keep on digging a while longer in the parched sands of mystery! Your kinsmen the diviners say that a little further down, just below the roots of the cypress and the rue, flows the pure and unfailing Spring.

Culture, like Abraham, has to wait a hundred years before it begets legitimate children.

If we would know the abyss of our ignorance, let us ask men of science to define in language that will mean something their own fundamental terms: Matter, Energy, Electro-magnetism, Life, Idea, Volition, Reason, Inference, or Generalization. They are left undefined; for the most erudite of us live by faith, and nearly all our knowledge if we follow it to the end is incantation. This faith rests upon a persuasion which precedes reasoning, therefore is not the result of reasoning. It consists in the trust that beneath our frothy words there is Solidity which is magnificent, and that it would rejoice and fulfill us if we knew it.

There is a python-type of mind which swallows knowledge in bulk—after first crushing it to death.

Many a man would be more intelligent if he were less intellectual.

We learn only what we have made ourselves fit to learn.

Sentimentality consists in refusal to scourge Knowledge with the whip of Truth.

The body cannot assimilate much poison. The mind can accustom itself to assimilating nothing else.

The incidental mistakes of genius cause joyous cackling to the mediocrity which never does anything to which a mistake would make the slightest difference.

Man has clear knowledge and dim vision. It is from the clear knowledge that his worst illusions spring.

The illiterate vulgarian has a great contempt for the highbrowed. But it is insignificant compared to the learned vulgarian's contempt for the high-minded.

That we should ever have been enchanted by the glitter of academic theories or humbugged by the intoxications of the flesh becomes to full-grown reason the most incredible feature of that swarming superstition, human life.

From the banquet of knowledge we depart stuffed. From the table of Truth we rise hungry.

Knowledge is a pitiable fragment and will ever be. It is something outside of its field, namely the will for Truth, that bestows upon it a dignity which it does not itself possess and invests it with a nobleness which no avarice in heaping up such fragments could possibly confer.

We do not read a novel or a play backwards from climax to introductory first page. But clever fellows among us are reading the story of man backwards and finding the key to its meaning in tadpoles and spiders. They are willing to ruin the story in order to disfigure the hero, to disorder a realm in order to discrown its king.

"Things" are the petty cash of Learning's trade in secondhand goods. They will be swallowed up one day by Spirit's magnificent monopoly.

Wisdom wearies people not because it is sometimes deep but because it is always sad.

The sceptic wears the breastplate of Faith, only he puts it on behind.

A sceptic is a useful person so long as he retains his amateur status. When he becomes a professional sceptic he is not worth the fee that he charges for the trick.

There are men who boast of a free mind who nevertheless allow only their prejudices to travel through it gratis.

Scepticism is a free spender—of money that somebody else has earned.

The highest vision leads us not to a moment of discovery but to the understanding that there is something eternal to be discovered.

When a man says "I doubt," that asserted self, "I," contains in principle the statement of all the affirmations and the resolving of all the doubts that are possible to Mind.

We could not rationally ask questions of Nature unless the answers were involved in the questions; nor could Nature satisfy the inquiry unless it were itself implicit in the inquirer.

Satan's best disguise is not Sophism; it is Sentimentalism.

A man's culture, both intellectual and spiritual, may be estimated by a very simple rule. Notice how many times in speaking of the opinions of others he uses the word "absurd."

If the student of the deeper things of the mind is seeking to know wisdom he may say: I am studying philosophy. If he is seeking to learn an apotheosized system, he must say: I am studying a philosopher.

Philosophy has wandered into many a disastrous aberration because in its principles and proofs it has taken no account of the deepest things of human life—which are not naked energies of Intellect, but aspiration, ideal trust, hope, and love.

In an inordinate love of the past there is something of the pagan despair that placed in ages long gone by the golden age.

Adopting a pose of sublime despair is a favorite defense-contrivance for having proved oneself unworthy or incapable of sublime ideas.

It is the tragedy of our age that in pursuit of intellect we have abandoned Reason, of the whole of which intellect is only one function.

Unbelief mourns over the soul's loneliness through misinterpreting that far profounder thing—the soul's uniqueness.

Man a rational animal? A ruinous definition! There can no more be a rational animal than a rational vegetable. Man is spirit working free from animality.

Nothing has a more impressive appearance of depth than absolute emptiness.

It is well sometimes to remember that what is time-honored may also be time-worn.

Both are wrong: those who think that nothing is to be learned from the past and those who think that everything is to be learned from it.

A tiger cub grows to adult tigerhood merely by time. But a human being cannot grow to manhood merely by time. What man's advance to maturity requires in addition to time is precisely the quality that gives to time its only serious significance.

Conceit of knowledge is the barbarism of the learned.

It will help us to understand how little the eye of science sees if we consider a heroic soul and an abominable blackguard. To science they are exactly alike. They have the same substance, and their physiological processes are to the last detail similar. Their chromosomes or electrons could be interchanged without making the slightest difference. The two men are rated by the same measurements, weighed in the same scales, and when ill of a like complaint are given the same medicines. To science they stand on a perfect equality. Yet one is hero and the other scoundrel, a world, a very universe of difference. Science takes no account of the only things that count most for human beings.

Scepticism murders all our certainties, and is satisfied only when it murders the will which derives its power from certainty.

Human beings are realized only when idealized.

When we are young we are concerned for what is in life. When we are older we turn our thought to what life is in.

Our age is confronted with this spiritual crisis: our new knowledge of the universe is calling for thought immensely enlarged while our minds have been narrowed by scientific and ecclesiastical theories and conjectures incredibly thin.

No one can live a life of thought without feeling either the woe of immitigable sorrow or the raptured touch of inextinguishable hope.

Do not blame the theologians too severely for not knowing where they are. Do physicists know where they are? Have they the remotest idea where they are going? Do astronomers know what their expanding universe is swelling to? Have political specialists any notion what the next move in social organization or disorganization will be? And out of the seething hash-pot of philosophy and psychology can the experts read any sign of what their To-day is or any omen of Tomorrow? Can evolutionists who possess an impossible knowledge of what happened fifty million years ago even guess, marvelous as they are at guessing, what life's next change will do for us? No: they are all at sea, knowing nothing except that the gale is high and their compass wrecked.

Yet over the whole tipsy crew the Pole Star shines, and about them is a sea that somewhere has a shore. If there has been any progress at all it must be because there is a Providence that takes care of drunken sailors and guides their zigzag blundering across chaos toward a haven. It is the theologian's merit to remind them that there is a haven and that it is not chaos.

4. Religion

Mir gaben die götter
Auf Erden Elysium
Ach warum nur Elysium?
GOETHE

"On me gods have poured by donation divine
The richest of gifts since the day of my birth;
Even Eden on earth they've allotted as mine.
Ah, why merely Eden, why only on earth?"

THAT the universe is communicant is the foundation of Science. That it invites us to communion is the pinnacle of Religion.

Faith is the vision of the realizable given to the unrealized.

Not to believe in Supreme Reason makes it at last impossible to believe in Reason as supreme.

A cosmos worthy of Spirit is necessarily appalling to Sense.

Why have men believed in God? Because to nothing else can the central soul give its loyalty, the Imagination its magnificence, and the heart's heart its love.

Better be servitors of a possible magnificence than parasites of an assured Triviality!

Man is never so incomprehensible as when materialism explains him; and never so luminous as when religion leaves him a mystery.

The object of our search for an ultimate Cause is not for a chronologically First, but for a necessarily Adequate; for a realization-place, not a resting-place.

Things existent darken the divineness of Existence.

Religion is reading the text of the universe in the Original.

Yesterday somebody died for honor. To-day somebody goes hungry because he is resolved to be free, forthright, and true. And still we are pawing in the muck of materialism and moaning over the inadequate proofs of the existence of God!

In the calculus of perfection one and One are one.

Mysticism is a non-stop flight to the only stopping-place fit for a being with wings.

It would be to our profit if there were more of the spiritual in our schools and less of the scholastic in our churches.

Mere being is donated to us. Kind-of-being it is our responsibility to return to the Giver.

Our daily needs make us practical. Our ageless necessities keep us mystical.

It is a fatal crack in unbelief that it admits a higher Law but denies a higher Realm.

The ecclesiastical dogma that man has fallen and the materialist dogma that he has nothing to fall from are kindred profanations.

When men cease to practise adoration they begin to practise idolatry.

If the calculation could be made it would beyond doubt surprise us how many of the godless base their denial upon the persuasion that to hold them answerable to Holiness would be a cruel and unusual punishment.

We struggle against the world that the soul is *in* because we would reach the world that the soul is *of*.

The man who says "Soul" with understanding can never live life in baseness nor leave it with fear.

The error of theologies is to give shape for all time to what was seen once in a moment that transcends time.

Extraordinary it is to see the amount of writing on Religion that is done by men who are too superficial to understand it, too dull to experience it, and too sentimental to abandon it.

One great difficulty in religion is the amount of slipperiness and unscrupulousness to be found among the professionally pious. And one great difficulty in irreligion is how obviously its professional advocates need religion.

Here is a noble paradox: Religion tries to satisfy man while its essential purpose is to make him dissatisfied.

Religion may call for a hard thing, faith in the dark. But Irreligion demands an impossible thing, faith in Darkness.

When God's exceeding light falls upon the world we may recognize it from the dusk and dimness that suddenly turn the whole fabric of earth to shadows.

Man's search for a divine revelation is the supreme revelation.

One Kingdom there is which we can possess only by giving up every other.

Superstition is virile poetry gone wayward among the imaginative. Irreligion is flat prose gone sour among the dull.

When the light in a man's soul becomes so dim that the deed of adoption originally written there is an illegible text, the Signature still remains a luminous Name.

What a loving God is, no church has ever taken seriously; for it requires the terrible understanding of what it is that God hates.

Irreligion is a system of therapeutics which would cure the eye-strain by putting out the eyes.

Loss of faith? There is such a thing. But let us stop applying the phrase to what is merely loss of nerve.

Some critics of religion take upon themselves the dirt which they scour from superstition.

There is in repentance this beautiful mystery—that we may fly fastest home on broken wing.

When men say: "The divine thought is too high for us!" their next complaint will be: "The divine deed is too hard for us!"

The fundamental insights of faith require and have undergone fewer transformations and corrections than the conjectures of philosophy and science.

With one single Companion the world is thronged.

The austere word of genuine religion is: Save your soul! The degenerate counsel of a counterfeit religion is: Salve your soul!

The radical fault of advanced religions is that they cultivate experiment before they have known experience.

Rate a preacher's power not by what he says but by what he has seen and does not say.

The religious genius is a man who would throw meteors, constellations, the whole scaffolding of Time, the green trees of joy, the withered trunks of sorrow, and the heavy crosses of sacrifice into one festival conflagration in answer to the mighty beacon that signals to him from the Far Beyond.

All religions rest at last upon the profound and tragic reflection: How woefully I need to be ennobled! How miserably inadequate this world is to ennoble me!

People who take religion seriously must expect harsh treatment from persons who take it professionally.

It is always a sign of religious decay when a faith begins to parse its poetry.

Heightened feeling tends to see the object that it longs for, even if it is not there. The soul in exalted moments discerns the splendor it was made for, even if it is not here.

If Religion only said to us: "I will train you to see!" instead of "I will teach you to recite what someone else once saw!"

It is strange that the mysteries of religion which are said to be above the highest reach of reason, are dragged down by theologians to pictorial formulations on the level of gross sense.

Shepherd your moral hybrids while you can. In the terrible veracity of the Day of Judgment there will be only sheep and goats.

We are blamed for constructing God in the likeness of our own inner life. Oh! that we were wise enough to do it!

Radical religion now wants us to stop adoring Deity and hoping for immortal life. Instead we are to centre our hope upon a pinafore paradise on earth, save man by slaughtering his soul, steal the stately language of old worship since the new evangel is incapable of stateliness, and mutter a few phrases of pseudo-science to prove our emancipation from recited creeds. No convert should be accepted unless he can swear that he is totally destitute of humor.

There are two kinds of doubt: one is born of darkness, Is it true? The other is born of light, Can it be true?

Knowledge of Nature is the end of scientific vision. Knowledge of moral nature is the beginning of beatific vision.

Anatomists study the dead for the sake of the living. Theologians study the dead in the hope of restoring them to the living. Religious geniuses study the living for the sake of the ever-living.

The faith that removes mountains comes from the vision that sees over mountains.

The mystic is a deep philosopher as well as a man of common sense. He knows that the dizzy tail-chasing of discursiveness and ratiocination has got to be put an end to sometime; and he gives it an end that *is* an end—Glory! And we may as well face the fact that he cannot be refuted by the inglorious.

The recognition of a Higher is absolutely imposed upon us. The recognition of a Highest is magnificently offered to us.

In Protestantism the religion of the Book is being replaced by the religiosity of the bookish.

It is because he stands in the shadow of the earth that the mystic grows giddy from the Sun.

The philosophers of cosmic despair offer us an arctic universe—with the auroral lights left out.

Evolution accommodates and adjusts us to every circumstance of our lot except one. Evolution has never trained us to accept death, though death is a common incident of every day and the one inevitable element in our mortality. Obliteration, extinction, nothingness we shrink from and abhor even when we imagine that we do not. This mighty divination and protest of the prophetic soul are the cry of reason for fulfilment, the answer of personality to vocation, the claim of the More-than-dust to a Greater-than-Time.

If existence leaped from no-life to life, why should it not continue its creative advance by leaping from life brief and broken to life consummate and fulfilled?

One unconfessed reason why some people deny life after death is horror at the thought of resuming the inane existence which they take into death.

To believe in dying is inevitable; to believe in death impossible.

Life everlasting is the correlate to Personality inexhaustible.

The end of a life which is moral cannot possibly be an ending which is physiological.

The Imagination, fiercely impatient for consummations, outraces crawling Time. The Soul, on fire for Vision, overleaps enshadowed Death.

Death will not extinguish us. It will do something quite as awful: it will show us the light that we have not been able to extinguish.

We may not fight a duel with Death nor engage in controversy with him. For he is not of our rank. He is a scavenger, skulks in charnels, and is the dirtiest of fighters. We must take the degradation of his final insult with scorn and pass on—with our faces turned the other way.

When Life has nothing of distinction Death has everything of extinction.

If we lived intensely we should die almost surreptitiously.

A scandal of thought should not be made a mystery of religion.

Bourgeois mediocrity never completes its perfect work till it founds a "religion of this world."

Jesus tried to hide his miracles, knowing that they would obscure his principles.

If we live upon magnificence we shall die into it.

The Christian religion has deposited upon the altar of wisdom the most profound and most beautiful set of paradoxes ever laid there: Defeat with lips to the bugle of Victory; Hopelessness burning with Expectation; Sadness radiant with Love; Darkness dazzled with Morning; Death shaken with the song of immortal Life!

Moses founded a religion of Law; Christ, a religion of plenitude of Being which no law can express, to be served by a fidelity of love the authority of which no codes of precept can ever equal.

If incarnate Word is a phrase too murky with metaphysics for you, substitute for it the valiant and accurate title, incarnate Fidelity.

For various achievements of self-conquest Christ promises a "reward in heaven," not in order to sentimentalize our cupidity but in order to rationalize our abnegation.

"Where two or three are gathered together in my name!" When were there ever any more? When will there ever be?

Landor is right. Religion is too pure for corporations. But, let us add, man is too impure to do without them.

We have two eyes, outer and inner; the one sees the dust, the other the quintessence within the dust.

Infallibility is not a great spiritual gift but a primitive sub-form of mechanism. The only infallibility that we know is of the instincts—the lowest part of us.

The honest seeker for a faith is only staggered by the intellectual difficulties of his sacred search. What floors him as he explores history is the moral crookedness of the men who say they have found the very treasure that he seeks.

The Prophet has a black-sheep brother but with a much larger following—the Dervish.

Creeds are cracked because inexpert and hasty potters moulded them. These apprentices would have been more careful had they realized that what leaks through the crack is religion.

One difficulty in religious institutions is their effort to make real what is past. Christ's method was to make what is eternal present.

The deadliest difficulty to theology is that much of it becomes intolerable when the human spirit grows mature, moral, and humane.

As we sometimes listen to the reading of Scripture in church the reflection comes to us that the Biblical visions of splendor which it is not lawful to utter, it seems nevertheless permissible to mutter.

At Christ's birth the glory of the angels singing in their hosts! At his death the roaring of a mob, the base compliance of an emperor's vicar, the smiles and taunts of malignant priests! Of the two it is these latter that yield to him the more magnificent tribute.

Physical Chaos was transformed to Cosmos by an uttered word. Moral Chaos is offered the opportunity of transfiguring itself to beatitude by an incarnate Word.

One of the paradoxes of the mystical person is his cry: "The night cometh when I shall see!"

A bit of early piety has a persisting influence. It saves the higher type of atheist from becoming merely a brassy ranter. The total absence of it makes the denier's despair theatrical when he means it to be tragic.

Whether there are miracles or not, belief in them is fundamentally a witness to man's invincible conviction that a sublime soul cannot be imprisoned in the servitude of mechanism.

A church is a lamp and should be proud to be. But let it not dare to think itself the Light!

Dante takes the soul of man seriously; Æschylus, Milton, and Shakespeare take crime seriously; the Founder of the Christian religion alone takes the universal loving-kindness of Deity as the consummation of existence seriously.

Religious institutions begin with a free experience too pure to last. They end with a dictated conformity too stifling for religion to endure or with a subtlety of evasion too dangerous for character to tolerate.

In nothing is the genius of the Nazarene shown higher than in his centring of existence upon love. For man's fundamental need is for ecstasy—and ecstasy is the canceling of isolation. It is together-withness. It is finding fulfilment not alongside of but actually in another. And such precisely is the central significance of Love. Love therefore is the very substance of Spirit, and if there is any Hell at all its midmost misery must be for the completely non-ecstatic, for individuals, that is, totally bounded by self. And its lowest level of woe must be for the self that feels some need of communion but seeks to satisfy it in something that does not fulfill but only more intensely limits.

Look back upon the world with History; look at it with Science; look into it with Poetry; look through it with Religion.

Creeds are sometimes sung in a church; in the heart never!

A god who confers no rapture is ruined. If his worship cannot be sung he is sunk.

The richest benefit conferred upon History by Luther and the Reformation is seldom mentioned. It is that when the Middle Ages were weltering in their last agony, when the standards and ideas of a thousand years were toppling to the ground, when anarchy in politics, in belief, and in morals was leaping like fire in dry straw over the culture of Europe, the Saxon monk and his mighty cause gave a spiritual principle to a world disorganized, a divine ideal to souls dismayed, a light for new achievement to an age overtaken by doom and despair. Protestantism, like early Christianity, redeemed a disintegrated era by freshly renewed and consecrated Personality. It faces another disintegrated era now, but the old passion is gone, the early daring devitalized, the first intrepid trust in the free soul's capacity for divine communion touched with the frost of fear. Heretic Protestantism is afraid of the heretic prophet. The cell of the text it finds safer than the orbit of the Spirit.

"In so foul a world as this," complains the Pessimist, "how can any man be touched with rapture?" "I'll tell you!" says the Poet. "I'll show you!" says the Mystic.

"Matter is embarrassed with Soul as a mystery or a freak," says the unbeliever. "No," answers the believer. "Soul is entangled with matter for discipline, valor, and overcoming."

Christianity has sublimely changed the nature of Sin from broken Law to violated Love.

A soul that can with any propriety be called mystical in the grand sense has two moments or phases. In one he is quiet, surrendering his whole being down to his faintest thought to an Omnipotent Glory of Righteous Will. In the other phase he is militant, bringing down his pulverizing hammer upon slippery churches, immoral states, brutal wealth, thieving confiscations, and corrupt schools. He is that awful apparition, hated equally by potentates and proletarians, an absolutely impartial man, who will not serve a human cause by servility nor a divine cause by lies. None such appears to be now on earth. But though you may miss him when he arrives because of his thirty years of hidden communion with his Sovereign, you cannot fail to know when he departs. There will be an earthquake again at his crucifixion.

With churches holding the legalistic formalism of apostolic succession as more important than the vitalizing possession of a Succession of apostles, wonder not at the scorn of unbelievers and be astonished no longer at the terrible words: "Depart from me; I never knew you!"

It will never be estimated how much religion has been injured by the intellectual impertinence of its doctors and theologians.

If you know all about the Trinity and the Incarnation and are clever enough to walk the razor-edge of orthodoxy so as never to fall into Sabellianism or Adoptionism or any other solecism of the catechism, I may admire your ingenuity and be stupefied at your knowledge. But if—O Grammarian of the Inscrutable—I have any concern to inquire what your Religion is, let me ask you: Have you ever had any moment of awe and glory that has cloven your life asunder, and put it together again forever different from what it was before?

Human nature a part of Nature? Not so! There is all the difference between them that there is between the demonic and the divine. Demonic is the necessitated mechanism of Nature's unity; divine, the originating creativeness of human nature's unit. In a constellation there is something of magnificent stupidity. In a soul's experience of sublimity through looking at a constellation there is everything of immortal wonder and unfathomable mystery. And how shabby the law of gravitation is compared with the unpredictable lawlessness of genius, imagination, and aspiration! Creation, not production, is the supreme word! It fits free spirit only and defies the choking clutch of the coerced and regularized.

When our up-to-date soul-engineers tell us that we should "sell" religion by the merchandizing methods so successful in distributing soap, tooth-paste, and cigarettes, they indicate that there is not enough religion left to be "sold"; there is only enough to be betrayed.

So Religion is only sex-sublimation! If so, the primitive tribes who make religion the most dominant concern and most rigorous authority that they have, must be marvels of continence and repression. But we do not find in savages so lily-white a loveliness! And furthermore, when all the parrots have duly recited: "Religion is sex-sublimation!" will at least one of them condescend to tell us how it can be made intelligible? Sex-passion translated into poetry, idealism, worship, and aspiration! There is no miracle of transubstantiation like it in the whole world. How can that root bear that blossom? And isn't it preposterous to say that it can? Blasphemous as the thought is, one fears that "sublimation" will have to be added to the heap of academic humbug that may be certified and guaranteed to asphyxiate thought.

You have discouragements enough, Reverend Preacher, and I would not add to them, but here is a fact that somehow or other you must fit into your ***Weltanschauung:*** You are preaching, let us suppose, at Mr. X's funeral, and you wish to say something that befits the solemnity of death, the mystery of sorrow, and the faith in immortality. Yet to Mr. X's associates who have gathered to hear you, nothing in his life is so significant as that he spent forty years in the glue business and was a good Elk.

Death is a renovating function of Nature.

"You must accept!" is the dictatorship of fact.
"You must conform!" is the dictatorship of creed.
"You must submit!" is the dictatorship of mobs.
"You must transgress!" is the dictatorship of hell.
"You must aspire!" is the dictatorship of God.

Barbarians and cultivated Græco-Romans confronted early Christianity, the Barbarians asking that the new religion should give them civilization, the Græco-Romans that it should cure them of civilization. The Barbarians desired a spiritual ideal that should purify their strength, the Græco-Romans, a loyalty that should invigorate their weakness. The Barbarians were the easier to treat, the Græco-Romans the harder to cure.

Theology has a mischievous itch to turn beautiful mystery into irritating puzzle.

The best proof of God's existence is what follows when we deny it.

Only in the lonely world of Spirit are we accompanied; in the thronged world of flesh we are bitterly alone.

An artificial hearth with a painted fire is what the Christian message becomes without the Christ-Messenger.

Churches perish from knowing too much about God and knowing Him too little.

We should not be too fearful that mechanistic theories of life will prevail. Mechanistic theories are confined to learned persons who are seldom entirely normal and never wholly human. As a matter of fact there is nothing that the spirit of man so detests and abhors as the machine and the mechanical when thrust into art and literature and love and joy. From that form of mud-dominion we may feel quite safe.

Faith, Hope, Love! And of this triad the one that calls for least faith is Faith.

A soul that strives through many failures is the nobler beauty than one too innocent to need striving or to encounter failure.

It would be enough to make me love God that He has let me know Truth: it would be enough to make me love humanity that some men have shed their blood for Truth.

The proposition that Religion is an empty thing because made up of wishes could come from no other than an academic source. Religion is built not of wishes but of will. It is precisely the authority that does most to chasten wishes, to control them, repress them, train them. Its advance is marked by increasing firmness in dominating wishes and by making ever more clear the distinction between the one-sidedness of primitive cupidity and the full demand of mature Reason for noble satisfaction. But the congenital weakness of the academician is to be distressed by will and scandalized at its insistence upon being recognized in a world-view and life-philosophy. This is too rugged for the consumptives of thought. So they take revenge by smirching the chief strengthener of will with a brush dipped in their own debility.

The petition of the infidel pessimist: "Tickle me with the assurance of demonic negation!" is exactly like the request of the superstitious Millennarian: "Flatter me with the promise of lush felicity!" Voluptuaries both!

To run away from the world is the poorest possible use for legs and feet. To fly away from it is the only possible use for wings.

Between God and man Pantheism asserts a metaphysical identification which cannot be avoided; Christianity prescribes a moral harmony which has got to be achieved.

Be a materialist, an atheist if you must. But open your eyes to all that it means. It means that you have no organic connection with mankind; that you are standing on air; that you are alien to the greatest art and profoundest experiences of history; that you have adopted a cause which, from having no past, can have no future; that you must ignore or suppress the deepest and most prophetic impulsions of your inner life; that you must accept as the fundamental tone and rhythm of your existence a tragic pathos that can never rise to victorious confidence or pure joy; and that you must regard the whole universe as a paradoxical imposture—a homeless home, a discordant order, a lawless abode of law, a systematic incoherence, a wandering without a destination, an ideal-fashioner without an ideal, a reach with nothing to grasp, links but not a chain, an unintelligent basis of all our intelligence, the blind bestower of all our seeing! If in sheer mental comfort and accommodation you find it easier to believe all that than to believe in Sovereign Spirit, no man can say you Nay—but do not expect the outraged universe to answer Yea!

CRITICISMS IN MINIATURE

Although the "Epigrams" were put in final order by the author, many of the "Criticisms" appear in print just as they came from his pen in the first draft and lacking the careful revision that he was accustomed to give the written word.

E. T. S.

Dante

The height of his great argument is, *come l'uom s'eterna*—when a moral person acts the act is forever. Mighty as the scene of his journey is, down the descending circles of appalling Hell, up the terraces of Purgatory quivering with expectation, and through the spheres of Paradise burning with the passion of infinitely realized and therefore eternally restless love, dominant over the whole tremendous setting is his single subject living out its full experience—inmost essential Soul. In that soul there is no play of motive any longer, no dramatic suspense or surprise, for it has arrived at its appointed and endless end. There is only the all-revealing vision of itself in frustration or fulfilment. The soul is heaven, the soul is hell; for heaven and hell are neither donated nor imposed; not allotted by divine writ nor fixed by any extrinsic act of judgment. The evil soul now on earth is in hell but cannot see it. Hereafter it will see itself as it is, and that seeing is essential hell. The right soul, high and true and pure, is in heaven here amongst its breathing fellow-men, but cannot discern and dares not guess the glory of its state. When it does discern it with other than human eyes, the discernment is heaven with its rapture of fulfilment and the blinding splendor of its Presences. So the most marvelous work of mortal genius spells out the lettering of Spirit, deciphers the text of moral Personality, and finds there the Everlasting and the superscription of the Ever-Living. Once we reach into Dante's meaning his mediaeval Italy passes away; the illustrious or obscure figures of old Tuscany and Umbria become simply dramatic moments in vast and superhuman consummations. Even his adored Virgil and his sanctified Beatrice fade to dimness in the exceeding light and we see him, an exile from Florence, a city then blind and heartless, and from the world, blind and heartless always, as an apocalyptic Presence unfolding the scroll of existence from Alpha to Omega, from the responsibility set for human will to the appointed ends implicit in divine law. Immense and sublime as the processes of this vocation are, they are never an artifice, never appear as simply straining after the Grand Style. The grandeur is not in the scene, nor in the author, but in the subject, the subject which he never lets go—Moral Soul. Dante simply takes Soul seriously as the centre not the embroidery of existence. That Soul is august. Its transcendent transactions spring naturally from its transcendent nature—

> . . . . . *questo cielo*
> *di me s'imprenta come io fei di lui*

—if I bear the stamp of heaven, heaven also bears mine. Never was there a mightier effort to tear the human spirit loose from fossilized frivolity. And if ever our dark night opens upon daybreak, Dante, the lonely pioneer of the regions of awe and glory, will be a guide to great-hearted adventurers who, having grown to spiritual manhood, will dare to seek a life-Cause fit for their sword and their stature. To those that stay dwarfed, those that take shadow for substance, those that have lost or scorned the supreme *ben dell' intelletto,* the final maturity of audacious mind, he has nothing to say. And in that haughty and sorrow-stamped face of his you may perceive that to such there was nothing that he desired to say.

Virgil

No man ever seriously read him without being made more deep, more true, more wise. He was so profound as to feel the pathos of life and history and of so lucid an insight as to understand that the *lacrimae rerum,* the tragic experiences of peoples, came from no fate arbitrarily imposed, but from frivolity and recreance deliberately cultivated. Remembrance of the heroic was woven into the texture of his soul—the first quality of a noble nature; and a sense of the unseen Dispensers of inescapable justice never for an instant departs from his capacious and contemplative mind. *Mentem mortalia tangunt* and the mortal things that touched his spirit bear the mark of contact with one of the loftiest and purest of the sons of men. He is a very marvel of a fitting pride of race, for he never permitted the pride to overleap the humble recognition of responsibility. In stateliness the first of poets; in restrained and modest admonition not far from the first of moralists.

American Poets

We are sprouting poets in America as though all our trees grew bay-leaves and all our breezes wafted music from aerial harps through all our kindergartens. But our songster-population, though they lisp in enormous numbers, utter nothing in mighty measures. For they have no sustenance, are not nobly nourished, know not the discipline and partake not of the faith without which there is no poetry and no poet of an authentic and commanding soul. They have read too much of the commonplace, these poets of ours, and in commonplace life are unable to see the grandeur forever withheld from common eyes. They wail, they moan, they pity, they rebel, but always as if frightened by what they conceive to be science and miserably deluded by what they take to be realism. The fierce independence of a great poet, his insistence upon his vision of the real as a vouchsafed insight into existence, his declaration of a faith toward which the tides of time must move, be contemporary Canaanitish materialism and academic parrot-squawking as arrogant as they may, his fire, his majesty of tone and assurance of vocation, in a word his seership, all are missed. Renunciation of the whole banal mediocrity of our age and its school is required of them, and with it a rebirth and adoption into joy and power and some sublimity of a faith. Until we have this kind of soul and seeing we shall have simply versemakers who try to redeem the pettiness of life by prettiness of words.

Abjure sociology and psychology, Poets, as you would cast aside a poisoned cup. Castigate as with iron whips the degradation of your mother-tongue which, *suadente diabolo,* the slipshod and the flat-headed have brought into it. Dare to think hard. Stop lackeying and valeting the spirit of the age. Cease apologizing for sublime visions and have courage to utter the word that has flown flame-fringed into your heart communicating rapture. Stand there singing, anomalous beings in whole colonies of unlearned and learned Philistines, not thronged but alone, not music-practising but divination uttering, taught by Beauty, and to Simplicity and a soul's sincerity bound by vows perpetual. Only so will the noble voice ever come, only so the strong hand that sweeps the mighty string.

Horace

THE darling of the dilettanti. He was capable of nothing great except perhaps great fright. In reading him one is conscious of polished art but never of profound substance. A glassy surface, a set of musical strings, a being sensitive to titillation, he never wrestled with anything, never thought out anything, never threw into his mind anything that keeps one waiting long for the tinkle of its arrival at the bottom. He plays with grave reflection, but it is only a prolusion; he is too near to the superficial and too close to the vulgar to mean it seriously.

Rationalism

Rationalism is a system that would arrive at the highest truth about Reality by concentrating attention upon the lowest revelations of reality. No seer, no genius of the first order, has ever lived who did not break loose from the reality conceived by rationalism. Genius would sink to commonplace if it did not. Shakespeare bounces off into a world of apparitions, portents, ghosts, and fairies; Aeschylus fetches in the Furies; Milton draws up his armies of the fallen and unfallen in prodigious array. Dante journeys through hell. Virgil leads Aeneas across the Styx and through Hades. Plato employs myths. Luke, the poet-evangelist, tells of choiring angels at the birth of Christ and consoling angels in his agony. Philosophical physics leaves the rationalist's matter-in-bulk far behind him, and describes the stuff as a mathematical probability that energy will be apprehensible to our senses and measuring devices at a certain world-point.

This is all scandalous to the good iron skull of rationalism, but it is a set of conceptions absolutely necessary if the Philistine is not to wreck the human mind and human culture. The Philistine wants to know if Shakespeare believed in "objectively real" fairies and ghosts. And it is fortunate that Shakespeare is not here to annihilate him by an explosion of laughter. Shakespeare would say to him substantially what the mathematical physicist would say, "There are spheres of Reality, and you cannot understand the lower until you subsume them into the higher. Your only objectivity is the sense-objectivity of maggots and mud. Of course my imaginative or mathematical forms have no such objectivity. I am not denying or even departing from mud-maggot objectivity. I am only probing into it, and as I do so I discover that it cannot itself be understood without a higher and finer context. For this context we have no vocabulary, since all vocabularies arise from the daily commonplaces of our Dagon-dense senses. I must therefore put my subtle perceptions into that coarse texture, just as you would put a seraph, if you saw one, in a tweed waistcoat and offer him a dinner of cabbage and pig's knuckles. Objectivity depends on what eyes you have to see with. I see in the conflict of souls super-material forces which I can represent only by the gross inadequacy of demons and ghosts. And you ask me if they are objectively real in your sense of objective! Blockhead, begone!"

But Blockhead has not gone. He still calls Shakespeare superstitious. He murmurs at the thinkers who have left nothing of his adored matter but a proviso, and in theology he will discourse upon the "objectivity" of the Nativity-angels and scholasticize into formulas of wood and iron the soaring soul of Christ. He sees the only world which eyes so muddy can see. The higher "objectivity" hidden and hinted at by the things of his thick pragmatism he is predestined never to see.

Spinoza's God

INFINITE fullness, but with the mass simply a heap admitting no discriminations of essences or distinction of values, might as well be absolute emptiness, a dimensionless vacuity, a zero of the size of Infinity. For such a monstrum we can have no possible love, since it has no capacity to receive love or to bestow it. Yet that dump of blank being is Spinoza's God, and when we are invited to offer it an *amor intellectualis,* we are obliged to answer that the heart cannot feel such a love nor the intellect conceive it. For love requires individuation and value, and conception requires specification and form. When anything is everything it is nothing. When distinctions are lost, anything that is left is certainly destitute of distinction, and most emphatically destitute of divine distinction.

Savonarola

A MAN for every age and ours especially to study. He is one of the immortal examples of a true man in a world of bounders, cowards, and squeaking spectres. The Renaissance era was his environment, prolific with pedants of a lipstick culture, thinking that they had grasped the soul of classical antiquity when they were incapable of rising above its embroidery and its poses. To these pretenders of the academic boudoir the chief sin was to depart from Ciceronian Latinity; the last of impossibilities, to have a moral passion, a profound thought, or a living soul of their own. Savonarola's ecclesiastical superior officer, and everybody else's superior officer, was a monster of perfidy and immorality; and a despairing or degenerate world had sunk into servitude beneath him. Then out of the consolidated imposture appeared this man to whom Truth meant authority and its service sacrifice, to whom Christ was not the *Giove crocifisso* of the clown-preachers of the age, but Master, Saviour, Martyr-king, obedience-demanding and hypocrisy-despising. In his desperation he made mistakes; in his ardor he forgot how foul the sewer was which his generation inhabited. But he refused to believe and obey a lie. As incarnate veracity, as an avenging instrument of Holiness on high, as courage superhuman and faithfulness unspotted, he is of the small company that gives us hope that diabolism will yet be defeated but Righteousness never. With his arms dislocated from the torture-chamber he mounted the fagots, had his quick moment of anguish from fire, and left to a world of liars an example that Time still dares them to look upon. There is a suggestion of earthquake rumblings in his very name, Girolamo Savonarola. There is a prophecy of Reformation and triumphant valor in his broken body and charred flesh. He is a holocaust to great Jehovah whom his brother-prophets of old Hebraism, who denounced the idiotic holocausts of a mummified priesthood, would have revered as an oblation worthy of the loving regard and remembrance of the Most High. Let him at least have ours!

Francis Thompson

No poet was ever admitted to a higher stall in the Seraphs' choir; and few mortals have ever lifted adoring song with voice of purer seraphic passion. But humanly wayward despite his exaltation, he sometimes mistook the Latin dictionary for the Seraphs' hymnal.

Walter Savage Landor

He wondered: "Why
Thorns live and roses die."

Thorns in terrible profusion he knew in his long fierce fighting life. But from the lacerations with which they tore his gallant heart sprang the roses of the noblest English prose of the nineteenth century, as if to answer his question or rebuke it.

Goethe

Ueberlebensgross und ganz original, myriad-minded—all words fail as predicates of his blazing, nimble playing, soaring genius. Give him but ecstasy and he would be the first of the gifted sons of men.

F. H. Bradley

A HEROD of logic, killing without mercy and with sombre and terrible joy! The corpses of half-thought theories litter the course of his avenging way; and the cadavers of some of the most illustrious celebrities of the nineteenth century are among the trophies of his wrath. As a logician, however, who knew the limitations of his science he slew only those who inadequately rationalized existence; but with fine divination he withheld his sword from those who spiritually experienced the Principle of existence. For spiritual experience was to him the Messianic Innocent whom a heavenly star might announce, whom wise men might worship, whom angelic presences might be commissioned to protect, whom therefore it would be sacrilege to kill. It was an experience which at its profoundest had been denied to himself. But he saw in it the vital energy of the Principle of being which a dialectic of the Absolute could discern only as a metaphysical shade, forced indeed upon the mind but not yet interwoven with the whole fabric of life. Before the Spirit's vision, not logicalized, not systematized but intuitive, immediate, and in the true meaning of the word ecstatic, he turned reverently aside, determined to be guiltless of profaning it. To many a student of his writings he opens a door to insight which he did not share, and points the way to conclusions which he left insubstantial and implicit. Like all Hegelians he is mighty in reasoning but infirm in moral feeling. Like all Absolutists he had a clearer view of the nature of existence than of the purpose of personal existence. A grave defect! Yet when all is said he is likely to stand at the head of the whole company of thinkers who have written philosophy in the English language. Indeed at his best he is not far from the foremost of the writers who have expressed themselves in English prose.

Freud

A Hebrew co-disciple of Augustine and Calvin—those other great specialists in the damnation of infants; and kinsman of the mediaeval demonologists who defiled the innocence of sleep with incubi, succubi, and other demons from the smokiest nethermost of hell. A complaisant science has taken from him loose and slovenly terms like "sublimation," "Oedipus complex," and "anal eroticism"; and a therapeutic method still in the witchcraft stage applies his incantations to the deciphering of dreams. These submissive disciples of his cure some obscure disorders indeed, but so do tattooed medicine-men, hitting a tin pan with a hammer at the bedside of their patient. So expert a topographer of the infernal realm is bound, when he speaks of human degeneracy and diabolism, to say much that is horribly true; but his resolute refusal to explore the super-ego, as his jargon calls it—that is, the region of our purest activities and inspirations—will stand in the history of science as itself an aberration dark with formidable omens. For when a man does not treat what is pathological as an aberrant incident in the history of health, but rather what is healthy as a puzzle or a freak in the history of disease, we have something more than a case of individual exorbitance and vagary. We have a symptom of an energumenous age, which is restless till it destroys and in torment till it defiles.

Den Originalen

Ein Quidam sagt: "Ich bin von keiner Schule;
Kein Meister lebt, mit dem ich buhle;
Auch bin ich weit davon entfernt,
Dass ich von Todten was gelernt."
Das heisst, wenn ich ihn recht verstand:
"Ich bin ein Narr auf eigne Hand."

GOETHE

Stout Fella!

Sir Bounder spoke, and his words were these:
"To no genius of old will I bend my knees;
I belong to no school, I acknowledge no master,
To follow a Teacher I count a disaster.
As for History, it's bunk, and traditions are dead,
And none of that humbug shall enter my head!"
O Bounder, if that is your path, boldly tread it!
And for being such an ass, keep unshared the whole credit!

Thoreau

THE most impressive instance in American literature of extraordinary power wasted in fantastic effort. Fantastic was his disdain of civilization; fantastic his adopting the hermit's external life without the hermit's interior vocation; fantastic his concentration upon self-perfection with no idea of the self-surrender indispensable to perfection. He had it in him to be the foremost man in the intellectual life of his country, but he was so absorbed in Number One that he reckoned all the other numbers as zeros, and there can be no leader if all the followers are nonentities. Nature taught his mind but human nature never touched his heart. Nature opened to him her secrets, but only her lesser secrets. She withheld from him the sympathy, humor, and pathos which raise the window upon the richest secret of all. Fishes would swim to his hand; but what was the good of that if no human heart dared lean upon his breast? A *saint manqué,* a priest of wisdom with a flaw in his ordination and an invalidating clause in his commission; an individualist with no recognition of the communion which protects individuality from arbitrariness and anarchy; a sage fallen short of graciousness and humility; a Yankee intruder into Olympian councils, too stiff-necked to observe the rules of creatureliness required for Olympian audience, and quite ready to argue before those august Principalities that Aphrodite, their regal form of divine beauty, had risen the day before yesterday from the ripples of Walden Pond. Let him have his cold niche carved of marble or alabaster! but the pity is that his effigy might have been the chief figure in the sanctuary window, mellow in the sunlight, and shedding the warmth of a benediction upon the worshipers in the shrine.

Our Teachers of Cosmic Despair

THESE emancipated persons, as they call themselves, must allow us to tell them how funny their tragic pose sometimes is. They take great pride in logic, have a grand contempt for the imperfectly logical, and stick a Mephistophelian feather in their cap for being themselves mercilessly rigorous in reasoning. Sentimentality they gnash their teeth at. Wish-thinking, as their very illogical and unmeaning term is, calls for an encore in teeth-gnashing. And as for Religion, *Conspuez.* The thing is for morons. Existence, they tell us, is idiotic. The universe is a monstrum containing a lure for our susceptibilities but smashing ruin for aspirations and expectations. There is no love in it, no heart. We love, we have a heart. We have dreams of grandeur. We wistfully stretch out our affections for beauty, joy, and peace. But the universe is a huge triviality, a Bedlam all howls, a swollen cruelty all devilish. Nothing is of any significance. Senseless destruction follows upon the heels of meaningless production. Science knows only events, perhaps it is not too anthropomorphic to say a course of events, a procession and connected train of events. But that anywhere in the events or beneath or above them there is anything that corresponds to purpose, to concern, to interest, to love and loving leading, is a superstition altogether abominable and calling for curses.

Therefore we are ruined. Our love will go down the red gullet of the dragon of being. Our hope is a morsel for his tearing teeth. Our momentary joy lives only till he swallows all the rest. Existence is for us a respite in hell. Life is a gleam in Erebus soon to be smothered in infernal night. Nothing matters since all is matter. Everything perishes since Doom is King. Horrible! horrible! horrible! This Shakespearean cry is the best and truest solution to the infinite insanity which is the universe. What then shall we do? Take the awful tragedy into our minds and make it at home there? Accept irredeemable despair! Hurl into the Gorgon's shapeless face invincible defiance! Then die and rot! So we shall ennoble our transit across the little span of life, proudly displaying the pageant of our bleeding hearts, and as blackness covers us we shall leave upon the page of our immitigable woe a last eloquent record of unconquerable contempt.

It is a stirring homily. Pessimism stands so near to truth that it strikes into resonance half the chords of our inner life. And defiance stands so near to foolishness and unreality that it has only to show itself to captivate a large part of the learned world. But as we look into the thing, the more weird as the product of logical minds does it appear. For first, if in the world of being there is only triviality, how can we give this gloomy magnificence to our forlornness and despair? If man is but an organic scum upon the surface of that inconsequential cinder the earth, what a distortion it is and how unreasonable for the scum to assume Promethean and Titanic postures! In plangent prose we are reminded of the sublimity of our sorrow. But by what right, when of sublimity there is none, and when the sorrow of us human midges has no more meaning than the flash of lonely waves on Greenland's icy shore? Where stars and galaxies exist and cease to exist unmeaningly, animate generations appear and disappear irrationally, where from top to bottom there is nothing at all but chaos howling in a void, how can we justify the sentimentalism of making our own paltry woes glorious in their bitterness and of splendid dignity in their defiance? Rhyme there may be in this singularity of stateliness, but surely no reason. If existence is the idiotic nightmare that these logicians say it is, then we are incidents in the nightmare and infected with the idiocy. From this conclusion there is no possible escape. If so, then to magnify ourselves by magnifying our griefs and to surround ourselves with the pomp and circumstance of noble pathos is most assuredly the last convincing proof of our idiocy. Grant that life is what Bertrand Russell asserts it to be and there is only one reasonable way of enduring our pain—namely to reduce, not exalt, its importance. Grin and bear it would be our logical maxim, but by all means grin. What else is there to do in a crazy cosmos? But of all inept things, the theatricalizing of ourselves into a strutting majesty is the most completely inept, the most radically sentimental, the most ridiculously artificial.

Cannot our princes of darkness see that they have become what they profess to scorn—angels of light? Can they overlook the plain fact that this denial of spiritual supremacy in the universe would lose most of its force and all of its eloquence if there were not implicit in it the affirmation of that supremacy? For what are they saying but that at the crown of existence is Soul, and that Soul is of greater significance and higher worth than the whole order of mechanism and the entire heap of material things and physical processes? That defiance to which they counsel us, that unbending aristocracy to which they summon us, that lofty dignity with which they invest us—amounts to nothing but wind unless the human spirit is actually exalted to primacy and unique prerogative. They set man's soul apart from dead things and iron law—this they acknowledge. What they do not acknowledge but in consistency should, is that they also set the soul above the world of things and the realm of necessitated law. Their scorn of all that such a world and realm can do is a sign of supremacy. Their disdain is a token of superiority. Their *non serviam* is a plea of higher status and immunity. Else it is buncombe pure and simple. But it is not buncombe. It rings too resonantly in our deep hearts to be that. This stupendous assertion of our loftiness, this approach to sovereignty over physical Nature means and must mean that beneath the emotional apprehension of our distinguished station there are in the nature of existence justification and rational foundation. A soul that is really trivial could not utter these protestations of lordly rebellion without being ludicrous. They are not ludicrous only because lordly we are. Majestic words cannot be put into the mouth of insignificance; for the more majestic they are the more foolish they would be. If we are to suffer and die sublimely as we are bidden by these men to do, it is nonsense unless there is sublimity in the nature thus highly preached to. Hence in the chimaera-world and Bedlam universe that we are told of there is at least one noble rational and moral splendor, man's soul. Our pessimists by their school logic deny it, but by their spiritual intuition affirm it. Now let them put their logic to work upon their intuition, and they will begin to extricate themselves and their disciples from the swamps of contradiction that they are bogged in at present.

Finally, have our philosophers of midnight thought out the significance of their constant relapsing into light? They defy the black stupidity of Nature. They will die, they say, in haughty protest against it. Very good. But if they lift themselves above Nature, toward what or into what do they exalt themselves? "Defiance of Nature," "above Nature," "protest against Nature" are quite appalling phrases to come from naturalists. Have the naturalists reasoned through the ringing rhetoric, or merely entranced themselves with its music? Can any sense be put into it if Nature, the big thick world of things, is everything? Not a grain of sense, so far as I can see. How can we defy it, or step loose from it, or rise above it, and across the dividing gulf hurl our scorn at it? Absolutely impossible! Once more the resounding words are all wind and all nonsense. The impossible cannot be made reasonable even by declamation. Yet, as I intimated, our sombre thinkers in straying from logic have lapsed into light. We can defy Nature, we can rise above it, but not on their principles. We can make this marvelous separation of ourselves from Nature only because we are, as essentially human, different from it and higher. The world of things is beneath us. Another world which we must call Spirit is above us; and to this world we as spiritual beings belong. With this understood—and every human being intuitively and invincibly understands it—we have a rational ground for defying death and for believing that we leave the world of death as conquerors. But the fine defiance of the naturalist rests on nothing. He cannot for all his poses meet death as a conqueror. He is its victim in the most complete sense of the word. He dies and sobs. What then is the good of his grand epilogue? No good at all. In the exchanges of contempt Death has the last word and it leaves of the rebel-philosopher nothing but a cadaver and clay.

Yet once again if the naturalist's logic rests on wind, and issues in echoing phrases devoid of substance, his intuition shows him the truth and irresistibly draws him to it. He cannot escape the conviction that rottenness is not a fit end-all for a being with a soul. He knows that it is by the irrepressible force of our spiritual nature that we defy the corruption of our physical nature. But having asserted his higher nature, he has not the remotest idea what to do with it. He finishes it with one last gasp of defiance which is, on the whole, worse than the last dissolution of rottenness. Rottenness is only physical decay; defiance is spiritual inanity and collapse. Rottenness might produce something useful in the physical world. Defiance is fatuous and useless in all worlds.

Joan of Arc

ONLY one Martyr may more justly be called divine. The python-pedants that killed her and the clown-king that lifted not a finger to save her have left their like on earth—plenty of them. But her like we shall not see again till faith and innocence and rapture appear once more to scandalize soulless schools and to move malignant blockheads to murder the inexplicably heavenly as they have ever done. She is a saint now; but she always was by a higher decree than a Pontiff's bull of canonization. Her true glory is dimmed by ritual incense and the ceremonial gaudiness of official processions. It is seen rather in an illiterate girl of nineteen telling the haughty doctors of the University of Paris and the iron-headed theologians of the Holy Inquisition that there was a learning which belonged to souls but not noticed in the catechism, and that by divine favor she had been privileged most marvelously to share it. Unearthly Presences had spoken to her, a divine calling been laid on her, and in the orchard of her father's farm at Domremy the Unseen, whose visitations cannot be confined to any one time nor monopolized by Palestine, had shed its wondrous light on her and to its exclusive and sacrificing service sealed and consecrated her. To that service she had stood true through the sneers of coarse ridicule and the shock of cruel war. Still steadfast to it she would die! When her time came some sanctimonious murderer lit the fagots heaped about her, blasphemously muttering the name of Jesus! She died with a great cry speaking that same sacred word, triumphantly sure of invisible and loving companionship to the last! That is her glory, all her own and not granted by any benefit of clergy, unearthly in wonder, a witness to the Mystery into which only the pure in heart have the divining eyes to see, but upon which our muddy eyes scaled to arrogant and materialized superstition may not presume to look. On May the thirtieth she died at the hands of clerical assassins. It is our Memorial Day. Who is worthier than the Martyr-Maid, the Virgin of vision but never the dupe of the visionary, to share in our remembrance?

Shelley

SONG incarnate—dwelling in a house of crystal after he had given sledge-hammers into the sturdy hands of Chaos and defied him to do his worst.

Carlyle

HE was happy in no companionship but that of Jehovah of Sinai. Tender as his heart was, and penetrating into every motion of the actors in the human tragi-comedy as his supremely artistic eye was, he laid upon himself the vocation of breaking the heads of men with the Tables of the Law. To that awful companionship and that tremendous doom he remained to his last lonely hour laboriously and fearlessly faithful. A prophet with even more to foretell than to denounce; an artist with so much to say that he cared not whether he became inartistic in saying it; a stormy contemplative who gave to silence more praise than observance! Yet however much he said, he told less than he saw, and he saw less than in the divinations of his unquiet heart he felt and feared.

Santayana

He is, not by his fault of course, unfortunate in his disciples. There have always been shallow creatures who are captivated by a philosophy of negation and who assume superior airs for professing it although destitute of the capacity for analyzing it. These are the empty beings who hailed Schopenhauer with a trembling *"Führer!"* and followed Freud muttering *"Maître!"* They are almost the unpleasantest bounders among the sons of men, an insect-growth bred from a faith in dissolution and a culture in decadence. They have been buzzing about Santayana too, thinking him far gone in the necrosis which they regard as emancipation. But to his credit he despises them, not because of their denials but because there is no imaginative dignity nor poetic pathos in their denials. They are in the mud but with no melancholy remembrance of the stars. They are rotten before they were ripe. And not for Santayana is precociousness or proletarianism! To the crude cubs of Godlessness he will not be godfather!

Yet it is not without a justifiable sense of affinity that they knock at his door for adoption. In no meaning of the word are they aristocrats; but in him they see a Latin disdain which gives to his thought the fascination of aristocracy, a Southern European sensuousness which attracts the impressionable who believe that poetic form is a substitute for spiritual substance; and a Catholic contemptuousness of pity for heretics which to the servile-minded confers the glamour of a Hidalgo's hauteur. To him myths are true provided that stupid literalists do not look in them for truth. Truth is an idol worshiped by serious imbeciles of Teutonic and other Northern peoples who take life grimly, who are not debonair, who senselessly dive into the ocean of mystery and drown themselves crazily when, had they saving romantic grace of the Latins, they might luxuriate in voluptuous moonlight and hear old Triton blowing on his horn! But is there a Triton? Only blockheads ask! It is as futile a question as Is there a God? Is there a soul? Is there anything transcendent in duty? Let there be fastidious satisfactions, and leave to heavy Germans the superstition of perfect fulfilments! Fundamentally, if we must speak of so gross a concern as foundations, the life of a spider is as significant as the life of a man. Snatch therefore from the flying hour what man may with distinction enjoy but what no spider, through the accident of spiderhood, can, so far as we know, possess!

If this is corruption, never was corruption put into prose so musical. If it is intrinsically frivolous, never was frivolity more elaborately constructed. If when we quench the sparks there remain only the sterile ashes of materialism, never was materialism so suggestive of mournful nostalgia for the altar light. Santayana is a poet who looks upon form with the delight of intoxication, and a philosopher who looks into the substance of life and thought with the short-sightedness of levity; and upon levity it is difficult indeed to bestow the crown of a monarch of thought without getting it awry.

Cardinal Newman

A SPENT force in religious thought, a lasting influence in English style. He pretended to understand scepticism though he never did; but did not pretend to understand democracy or liberalism in any form, for he so thoroughly and peevishly hated them that he never dared venture the pretension. His cure for scepticism was the most ineffectual of all—the saccharine treatment; and his anodyne for the pangs of liberalism was the most unpalatable of all—Tory antiquarianism. When during the Vatican Council of 1870 he opposed the definition of the dogma of papal infallibility, instead of openly supporting the bishops who were valiantly fighting the new dogma on the floor of the Council, he betook himself to invoking Athanasius and Augustine, Gregory and Ambrose that they might avert the disaster of this addition to the Creed—an ecclesiastic's manoeuvre rather than a soldier's decision. To a soldierly conscience indeed he has little to say, and to a modern seeker for a faith, nothing. If he had spent some of the time that he devoted to the Greek text of Athanasius in learning German and so acquainting himself with historical science as applied to the Old Testament and the New, he might have done a service to religious inquiry, though it would have been at the peril of his peace. Lord Acton's description of him as the manipulator rather than the servant of truth is indeed severe; but it is not unjust to say that his subtlety in accommodation puts the silencer on the forthrightness of his moral sense. There is a wail in his voice—but it has become one of the lingering cadences in the music of English prose.

Mr. Lippmann as Philosopher of Morals

Mr. Lippmann has done something which it must have been difficult to do—written a treatise on morals without the slightest effort to explore the moral experience from inside. He speaks constantly, however, of "maturity" and the "mature mind." But what this presumably valuable and rare acquisition is, he nowhere fully informs us. The inference seems to be not extravagant that the mature mind consists in having gone to Harvard, in having got hold of a foggy notion that science has destroyed the primary spiritual certainties of man, and in having seen Santayana plain. Impressive as these advantages are, they have an appearance somewhat provincial and raw. Certainly they are not an adequate substitute for philosophical depth in treating one of the profoundest of philosophical subjects. And as for "high religion," the name that Mr. Lippmann bestows upon the fastidious Stoicism that is to replace the religion now existing in minds not yet mature, one is forced to wonder whether Mr. Lippmann is not the only professed and converted member of it, and whether if his own principles were logically carried out, he ought not to excommunicate himself.

Lord Acton

Forget if we will the immensity of his learning; his courage in braving the dread name of heretic; his lifelong and adoring love of liberty; his purity of life and humility of heart. But one thing in him let us never forget, his invincible and intransigent assertion of the supremacy of moral law! No other man so richly deserves the title, let him therefore wear it: he was the incarnate conscience of the nineteenth century. Before successful crime he stood unmoved by its success, the inflexible judge of its manifest wrong. In the presence of the serpent sophistry by which crime points to its good results in excuse for its foul means he uttered a human indignation that seems to ring with the anticipated austerity of divine wrath. To the corrupt kings and prelates who violated the Higher Law, and to the clerical devil's advocates who explained away the iniquity, caring little whether by the same act they did not also explain away the God who forbids iniquity, he addressed the blasting denunciations of a moral passion that would not harmonize heaven and hell nor believe that Deity can be served by lies. An age of compromise, of moral scepticism, and of practised art in degrading the highest of all values into the service of the lowest of all compliances, was startled to see in him a soul that took seriously the obligation of a soul, and with jealous loyalty kept for his Everlasting King the chief subject-offering which that Sovereign demands—a conscience unperverted. In comparison with him Carlyle is of rudimentary moral perception; Newman is subtle and slippery; and the ecclesiastical diplomats who plied their devious trade in order to discredit him are of the value of a cloud of gnats.

He knew too much and was too scrupulous to write extensively.

But his literary infertility but leaves him more majestic in his splendid eminence as an Exemplar of Right. Happy the young scholar who, living in the miasma of the schools, makes acquaintance with this embodied moral healthiness, this robust sayer of Yea and Nay, this Dantean soul, this genuine man, whose very voice and presence made it impossible even for a run-down age to forget altogether that Justice and Truth eternal still exist!

Browning

HE wrestled so strenuously with problems of thought that his muscles became too tough and his manner too harsh for the fragile delicacies of rhythm and rhyme. But there were hardy and beautiful flowers that did not wither from the grasp of his sinewy hand; on his athletic shoulder at rare moments the lark would perch for song; and in the vivid flash of his eye shone the soft light of communicant stars. The first impulse of criticism is to apply to him not poetic standards but moral. For the promptest word that comes to mind as one reads him is not for his prosody, his subtlety, his eloquence, nor even his marvelous fecundity and inventiveness, but for his valor and veracity. No wholesomer and sturdier man is known to poetry; no poet of more rigorous loyalty can be found among the servitors of Truth.

Go in Peace!

Look in upon the cold respectability of a Pharisee's dining-room! The saints at table, ever vigilant for propriety, are uneasy, and this day are sitting on the edge of alarm. For they have an unconventional Guest and they fear that He may break out at any moment with another of His violations of the strict observances which keep the saints holy, protect them from seeing too much or too deeply, and safeguard them from any irrational generosity in loving. And now comes scandal, sudden, brazen, wholly horrible! A woman low and impudent and, in the worst sense of the word public, flings herself in upon the party. Before anger can cry its protest or outraged decency summon force for her expulsion, she is at the feet of the Guest, weeping upon them as she shakes with sobs, and softly stroking them with her long loosened hair.

"Stay, Simon," says the Guest to the quivering host whose house has been profaned and whose religion desecrated. "She loves, therefore she is cleansed. She has bathed my feet with tears and kissed them. She has braved your wrath and her own shame to come near me and prove her trust in me. The Father purifies a heart so generous. And, Daughter, a word to thee! Thou art white and beautiful and forgiven utterly. Degrade not love again! Go, great loving heart, in peace!"

In the whole chronicle of aged Time there is no incident like this. In the whole disturbing record of the ten or a dozen men of history who deserve to be called saints, no chapter shines with a light so unearthly, so marvelously profound and pure. Close the dull tomes on justification and redemption! Fatuous all! This woman knew nothing of their lore nor did this Guest; yet where the pedant theologians mumble and stammer, she is articulate with the tragedy of earth and He with the eloquence of heaven. Degrade not love any more! But love with all the might of thy heart! Love humbly, wistfully, even hopelessly! It is just so that God himself loves. Wait thou, O frustrated, beaten, broken heart —wait for the redeeming vision—it is near; wait for the bestowal of the immortal peace, it cometh to be forever thine! The

faces of the elder years,
High souls absolved from grief and sin,
Leaning from out ancestral spheres
Beckon the wounded spirit in.

Ruskin

He grew his lilies on the slopes of Sinai and on awful Horeb heard the lark.

Oswald Spengler

He has a *Weltanschauung*—a world-view—that is immensely impressive, but a *Lebensanschauung*—a life-view—that is deplorably emaciated. The world of history to him spins down the slope of absolutely incurable and inevitable decadence till it sinks in the bog of futility at the bottom and gurgles to extinction. But the same monster—Destiny (*Shicksal*)—that rolls every civilization to doom, draws to the top of the slope from some mysteriously fecund source of being, which is very obscurely described, successive new civilizations, young, beautiful and creative, to flash forth in brief splendor till the gravitation of fatality pulls them in their turn down to predestined destruction. Like Freud he is a specialist in pathology and death but has no word on the significance, the resources, the vitality, and the moral power of Persons. We ask in vain from him why the vigor of young civilizations cannot be kept in old civilizations, and whether intelligent will cannot renovate a society since the unintelligent thrust of unaccountable Fate never fails at the exactly appointed hour to create one. But no; he sacrifices a *Lebensanschauung* in merciless consistency to his Moloch-*Weltanschauung*. Character, responsibility, and retribution are hurled into the mechanism of his prodigious Law of changeless change, the feudatory of Death but inexplicably at the same time the ministrant of Life. Only an age with the memory but not the experience of faith, an age that looks to despair for heroism but not to Hope and Life for joy and victory could have produced this mighty mind, and only the frivolous can ignore the dark portent of his appearance.

Evolution

Evolution is an idea that requires a drastic and sceptical analysis. As popularly and even professionally held, it is alive with absurdities which are a disgrace to science. How can we regard evolution as consisting simply of next-steps in lineal continuation of preceding steps? Reason asks the irrepressible question: How and whence came the first step? For long ages there was in animal life no such thing as an eye. What rational meaning can we put into the statement that eyes are the next-step from no-eyes? that vision is a development of non-vision? And when oxygen-carrying corpuscles first appeared in animal blood, is there any sense in saying that red corpuscles are an evolution from no-corpuscles and oxygenation by the blood an outgrowth from oxygenation through the skin? Vision was an innovation since there was nothing visual from which it could have proceeded; oxygen-carrying corpuscles were an abrupt arrival since blood had been totally destitute of them before. And the assimilation of foreign substances as food was an innovation coeval with the mighty apparition of life itself. It is impossible that it should have evolved, since there was nothing from which it could have evolved, and life would have perished while waiting for it to evolve.

Whether we can rationalize it or not by our puny formulas, which are pitiably inadequate to reality, it is novelty, sudden appearance, the impromptu arrival of a higher, that gives a basis to evolution and makes its progress acceptable and even accessible to reason. The presence of a new perfection cannot be linked to the total absence of that perfection; an advance cannot hop out of the entrails of stagnation, a life-form cannot have a parental generation from a zero.

And as in biology so in history. Luther was not a next-step from preceding reformers or from popular discontents. He used them certainly; but his stature is his own, not theirs. He is a creative man, not a "little more of the same," not an inheritance nor an adaptation. And Shakespeare read, let us say, the Greek tragedians, the mediaeval mystery plays, the English poetry of an earlier day. But does he merely continue these types? Does he simply add a fresh accent to their speech and a new chapter to their text? Obviously absurd! Shakespeare is an apparition, as genius forever is; he comes as a new thing, not as a specimen of an old thing somewhat "evolved."

Nor was Jesus a next-step. He did not just carry forward by one foot or one mile the journey of Judaism. He was not a Jeremiah with an accidental variation added, nor an Isaiah with a more tender heart or a more penetrating voice. An innovation he was in the sublimest sense; and no calculus of analysis can find him hidden in his geographical or historical antecedents.

The effort in fact to reduce all differences to some distant uniform minimum from which later perfections are to be magically drawn out is bankrupt. Nothing little by taking steps can ever cease to be little and become great unless a principle of greatness operates in it from the first. A uniformity destitute of qualities cannot originate a new manifoldness profuse in differentiations of quality. The universe refutes our closet rationalizations and our kitchen diagrams. We live in the bosom of Immensity—and the Immensity is not dead nor parsimonious. From its abyss of riches it hurls into our time-world its treasures by its own mysterious dispensation, not by an academicized time-table. Evolution means the lengthening story of its bestowals, its uncoverings, and its manifestations of creative fecundity, every one of them a token of power and a gleam of prophecy. Regularity, rationality, and coherence there are. The root however of the rationality and the principle of the regularity are its own august secret hidden in the unfathomable sea of its potency and purpose, but not revealed in our incredible superstition of maximum-out-of-minimum which travesties the stupendous process. Eternal activity forever originating, forever surprising, forever fashioning: an Incomprehensible lifting us to comprehension, but leaving with us wonder, humility, and expectancy, is the foundation of existence and the Awakener of those other unheralded apparitions—hope and awe and beauty and worship.

Rodin

HE used the medium of the most individualized form of expression that we have to picture forth the vast brooding universal mystery which no individualization can do more than foreshadow.

John Dewey

An accomplished player upon the philosophical instrument, technically correct, learned enough, inspired never. First principles do not much interest his cash-and-carry mind, and to his Yankee democratism, which is humanitarian rather than human, there is something offensively aristocratic in brooding upon the mystery of existence. To his thought a brooding hen is more useful as well as more suitably proletarian. Of all men alive he is possibly the most completely destitute of the mystical sense or of the sense and significance of the mysterious. His reverence therefore is acquired not native, assumed rather than felt. His world is small; and when, equipped with measuring devices suited to its smallness, he steps out into the vast universe of thought, it must be said that he is not likely to be long visible in its mighty spaces. He can stimulate action but he cannot reach up to the highest implications of activity nor confront the problem of the irrationality of mere activity. A philosopher of this world but not of world pure and simple! Such a world as he has is without a firmament; a pocket-world in which shrewd men feel for what is in the pocket, caring not at all from what mine or treasury it has got there; a breezy world but empty of atmosphere; extensive but devoid of perspective; a world of the sharp-sighted but the near-sighted, of the muscular but not the sturdy, of the regularly fed but the inadequately nourished. Only America could have produced him, and if he is an instrument of its present practicality and if it receives from him a satisfaction of such needs as it is now able or fit to feel, that, on pragmatic grounds, is justification for his existence and the best vindication of his enviable celebrity.

Chesterton

THE hugest playmate that ever romped with fairies and the aery sprites of merry mischief! But the most perilous also—for in his hilarious gamboling with them he sometimes treads cruelly upon the delicate feet of one of the Shy Sisters whose name is Truth; and his roar of leonine orthodoxy frightens into headlong flight another little leprechaun called Common Sense. And this is too bad; for the Small People have whispered into his big head such secrets of far-off wisdom and such endearments of elfin love as have been bestowed upon no other man of this heavy-hoofed age. When the Wee Folk foregather in woodland session to talk about him, Ariel questions but none of them can answer: "Why does the man argue so much with the fools of an hour? Why does he light so beautiful a candle and cover it with a bushel of controversial pamphlets and manifestoes? Why does he darken his scintillant humor by carrying it into the black night of a humorless and contentious partisanship? Why doesn't he stick to poetry and with our cousin-seraphs sing immortal songs?"

A Bulldozed People

THERE is a spacious American scene. But hardly discernible is the American soul that should quicken it. We should have a soul, a positive and unmistakable soul. We inherit liberty, the parent source of souls. We have not been niggardly in sacrifice for it—and sacrifice it is that gives to souls the seal of authentic adoption. By every right this Republic should lift itself from geographical expression and from external polity to spiritual figure and delineation; and upon the inner life of every one of its citizens there should be observable the stamp of a freeman aware of his country's calling and character. Yes, it should be so: the thing does not admit of argument. But it is not so. This immense area and enormous multitude show no light of an indwelling Spirit, appear to be stirred by no sublime remembrance, nor fortified with resolve to achieve an urgent and noble calling set for us by the destinies that mysteriously choose and jealously judge this earthy instrument.

The European and Asiatic peoples who have emptied out their hordes here, some of the best of mankind and some of the worst, have made it impossible for us to have a soul. We are allowed to have only a set of compromises and timidities which may never lose sight of the hatreds and race-conflicts imported from the old world. But to speak as an American with only American interests in view on matters involving these foul importations has become impossible. Suppose a man desired to study the effect upon American life of the Polish or Bohemian parochial schools with their preservation of the ancestral languages and their unsympathetic regard for the tongue, the customs, and the country of the Yankee heretics. What a hurricane would smite him, Know-Nothing!

Bigot! Xenophobe! Suppose he wished to inquire into Catholic canon law as offered to states, and estimate the likelihood of Papal aggression here as well as in England, France, and Germany in other ages—the theological pot would pour out its pitch upon his unfortunate head, and no pot ever held pitch more defiling. Suppose again that he studied American cities in which Irish politicians are supreme in power, and did his best to judge impartially for his country's sake the political morality of Irish majorities in our large towns. What a scream of celestial wrath from Hibernian souls! How deep the Donnybrook curses vented upon his black heart!

To end the suppositions, imagine another American carrying his researches into Jewry. He wishes, let us say, to come to accurate knowledge regarding the Jewish influence in revolutionary movements in this country or regarding the feelings toward this Republic that prevail in this or that college where Jewish students preponderate and are being given a higher education absolutely free. What a howl from Palestine! Anti-Semite! Judenhetze! Barbarous enemy of Israel and Jehovah!

No, an American soul amidst these insanities cannot exist. Newspapers and publishing houses know the lynch law of the terrorism from long experience and tremble lest the mobs roar at their doors. We wear chains forged in Asia and Europe. Politicians wear them proudly; the rest of us with the shame of slaves who remember that once we were free. For the purpose of declamatory lying our orators still bellow against capitalism for dominating the press. They know better if they know anything. The suffocating grip that is laid upon free inquiry and American independence in public utterance is not financial and domestic: it is racial, sectarian, and alien. But it has pretty thoroughly tamed us. We are indeed one of the best-tamed populations that the history of servitude ever knew. We are tamed into allowing corrupt laws to steal our property; into accepting as inevitable organized plunder groups that lift as much as they can carry from the public treasury; into accepting the reproach of educational charlatans when we venture to examine the schooling given to our children; into letting the constitutional privileges of free citizens be destroyed by the enemies of freedom; and into submitting to the treatment of moujiks and coolies sent upon us by the congressmen whom we maintain in their offices and emoluments. A bulldozed people, shaking with the ague of the terrorized is what we inheritors of independence have become; and intellectual liberty, the fundamental possession of a civilized society and our one remaining protection against the dictatorship which vicious gangs have determined to fasten upon us, seems about to vanish in the mass of compliant surrenders that mark the abnegation of our national inheritance. America's fight against Europe at its worst and Asia at its blackest will not be fought with artillery; it will be fought on the field of ideas and character. And unfortunately our education is weak in ideas, and neither our schools nor our churches are vigilant sentinels of the perpetually beleaguered citadel of character. Already an American solicitous for his country, forthright in speech and fair in method and temper, is hooted by alien blackguards as a Fascist. How long will it be before the curtain falls on the saddest scene of recreance known to time?

Our Learned Class

THE mediaeval canonists invented for the Pope an exalted prerogative which was expressed in the legal axiom *omnium mortalium judex, sed a nemine judicandus.* "He is the judge of all men, but no man may judge him." Our high priests of learning in this country have not actually appropriated this beautiful maxim; indeed—let it be spoken delicately!—a good many of them could not translate it. But the spirit of it they have appropriated and the haughtiness of it they have thought it no extravagance to assume. For whenever one of us who belong to the anonymous mass called the unprofessional laity ventures to murmur his astonishment or concern at some particularly outrageous piece of nonsense uttered by a learned professor, he is reminded of the immunity of pedagogues, charged with an assault upon science, and held up as a sort of racketeer feloniously attempting to break into the exclusive monopoly of truth-seekers. In point of fact he is fortunate if it is not insinuated that his mental age—and nobody not a professor has the remotest idea what that occult if not nonsensical mystification of chronology is—must be reckoned at eleven and a half. Is it wholly hopeless to inform the pontiffs of the universities that when judicious persons once in a while criticize them and are impatient and wearied with the wilder section of them, they have no intention of coercing them or of limiting the liberty of science? Have they a sufficient remnant of humor to understand that others besides the technicians of education are supposed to enjoy a modicum of liberty also and have as great a reverence for truth as anybody who wears a tassel in his cap and a scarlet hood upon his back? Will their touchiness not admit the thought that parents who are careful in selecting doctors to care for their children's bodies have a right to be vigilant in selecting teachers who will influence their children's minds and souls? Or will they go on in the spirit of the *judex omnium a nemine judicandus,* eloquent upon their prerogative but silent upon their responsibility, as persons of sharp minds and arrogant nature but infirm judgment and weak will always are?

The pretension indeed to exceptionally dispassionate intellectual equity and to even-minded impartiality in seeking Truth and manifesting truthfulness is largely humbug. The dons are very numerous who are propagandists pure and simple. These men are seized with some superstition social, economic, philosophical, or anti-theological, and make use of their office and its opportunities to hammer it into juvenile minds as a dogma not to be doubted. The perfect justice of an intelligence which sees but does not squint is as rare among learned specialists as among the thesis-ridden and theory-saddled true believers of the street and the soap-box. Who that has any knowledge of our lordly faculties can doubt it?

Nor does it admit of question that our learned orders display a lurch to materialism, and the cruder the materialism the more pronounced the lurch. A few years ago there arose a hullabaloo about behaviorism. If there was an uncooked and slapdash theory of human nature, behaviorism deserves to be called such. Yet the thing ran through our colleges uproariously victorious. European scholars looked on stupefied at the credulity and crassness of our high teachers, and although themselves hardened enough to materialism, they found it a scandal hardly credible that Americans presumably trained to fine discrimination and critical delicacy should gulp down food so gross with an appetite so primitive. And as for the Americans who take any interest in culture and scholarship, nothing that has ever happened in the intellectual history of the country so rudely wakened them as did this uncouth and hysterical canonization of the behaviorist creed to the barbarous ineptitude that may be housed in homes of learning.

Along with the vulgarizing of mind we cannot but observe in these dignitaries a vulgarizing of taste and manners. Professorial English would draw iron tears down Pluto's cheek. Surely some of the chalk-dust of culture should have clung to them from leaning against so many blackboards. But where can we find a grain of it in the harsh, twisted, club-footed style which they have accustomed us to expect from them? And what an act of faith it requires from us to believe that an exquisitely organized and graciously disciplined mind exists beneath so common and coarse an utterance! Worse still is the low and indecent disposition which has begun to claim right of asylum before the altar of science. We have all heard of the blackguard questions put to certain women students under pretense of scientific research. We have heard too of the extremely complaisant opinions ventilated from the Chair upon sexual conduct, and we have not been destitute of proof that these notions of debonair laxity have been put into disastrous practice in the shadow of the Chair. It might be reckoned to human frailty and foolishness that in a single coeducational institute of learning eight young women students died of abortion in one year's time. But it cannot be so easily set aside that their illustrious guides adopt and announce theories of life and conceptions of human nature which would remove from the path of the young any troublesome obstacle of dignity or valor or reverence or responsibility.

In fine there are American parents, more of them than we know, not by any means reactionaries nor afraid of modernity, whatever that obscure and swollen word may mean, who live in daily apprehension lest the wholesome sons and daughters whom they commit to a college return to them as brazen fools without culture, without habits of study, without a country, without common sense. And as long as such a condition of things continues as serious as it is now, we of the dumb laity may sometimes have our tongues loosened and may speak. We do not ask for impossible things. We ask only that our teachers be cultivated gentlemen and judicious scholars, nothing more. But after all these may be impossible things. For it takes a long time to produce any kind of gentleman. And as for cultivated gentlemen and judicious scholars, something immensely more rich and stately than vast pedagogical factories is required for begetting them. While we await them we who have long been patient may venture to advise our celebrities of the academy to be humble and perhaps even penitent. But this is another impossible thing!

The Ecclesiastic

THE ecclesiastic, orthodox or liberal, seems too far gone to be cured, too hardened to be converted. He insists upon iron formulations for the essentially free and the inherently intuitive; and he flies to short-cuts, to magic solutions, to millennial substitutes for merit and responsibility. If orthodox he will propose a creed weird in words, tangled in thought, and moldy in morals as representing the simple, true, and lucid soul of Christ. And if liberal or radical he is no less exorbitant and fantastic. Karl Marx has given us the gospel of the Lord in practical proposals! The Bolsheviks are exemplars of Christ's fraternal love! The "democratization of industry" or the abolition of the "profit system" will put an end to the anguish of the ages and stay the immortal soul's unrest! And all through the noisy and commonplace business is the appeal to the patronage of the Nazarene as though he too were a prim pedagogue or an itchy reformer!

It is beyond hope to persuade such men that the Master of us all gave no programme, time-table, or surveyor's map for any millennium, celestial or terrestrial, and that he would at once fall from his sovereign station to the paltry place of a mystagogue or thaumaturge if he had done so. He offers us rather principles of perfection terrible with the authority of love and beautiful with the assurance of hope. He calls us to an inward life purified enough to partake of that love and valiant enough to pursue that hope. An interior life first; and then such sad labor as we can spend for making our corner of the world conform to it! Christ's first and last concern is for souls; the ecclesiastic's for schedules. The schedule may be Nicæan and Chalcedonian tritheism, or Marxian materialism or Muscovite despotism. Some kind of schedule at all events he must have, a myth stiffened to a mythology, a vision destitute of seership, a kingdom more anxious for authority than for loyalty, more concerned for its sceptre than for its King.

Anthropomorphism

Taking fright at the word "anthropomorphism" has become a shallow and ridiculous fashion. Were we not anthropomorphic we could not think at all nor have a universe or a self. When a scientist speaks of Force he uses an anthropomorphism drawn from the act of will. When he says "Cause and effect," he employs another taken over from Purpose. When he talks of Law he adopts still another derived from reason and its regularity. When he mentions attraction, repulsion, and affinity, he manufactures another taken most manifestly from the affections and the heart. A universe not anthropomorphically described and interpreted would be to Anthropos the man inherently unintelligible. What a true thinker should set his mind upon is the impressive fact that the anthropomorphic is the cosmomorphic and the cosmogenic. And his chief fear should be not that he thrust upon the universe what is originally human but that he miss in man what is intrinsically universal. The intrinsically universal it obviously is which alone can lead us to anything true or significant about a universe. And distrust of what is universal in the interpreter destroys the universe which is to be interpreted by the interpreter. It is the transiencies and localisms of individuality that are not to be allowed to predicate themselves of the universe. But the universalities of essential personality cannot by any torment of manoeuvre be kept from substantiating themselves in the universe and from substantiating the universe in themselves. The universe is in our likeness or it does not exist. And we are something more than its product or could not exist. The universe is an adjective of mind. And we who possess mind, or are mind, partake of the aboriginal substantiality of the Subject Noun or Pronoun which gives actuality and meaning to the adjectival. The universe is not impoverished but enriched by being anthropomorphic—i.e., of man-form. And we are not romanticized but rationalized and realized by believing ourselves to be fundamentally of mind-form, and therefore kindred to the eternal and creative Principle of all forms.

What Is the Matter with Matter?

We have no profane intention of planting a precipitate foot in the cathedral close of sub-atomic physics. That holy ground is haunted, and the cloistered men of mystery who live there and are trying to materialize the spectres that swarm in its impalpable ether are not kindly disposed to coarse intruders unacquainted with the mathematical dialect which this kind of spectre speaks. Our simple purpose is to reflect upon what the men of mystery tell us has become of matter. For the stuff has disappeared, drifted off like cigarette smoke through an open window. And we who were reared in late nineteenth-century scientific orthodoxy cannot let matter go without fearing that we shall have to go with it. Everything is matter, we then were told, and having been told so we believed it. We even believed that matter way down in the heart of it had for final constituent something called an atom. An atom was the minimum of matter. You could not break it up into smaller bits. There it was, the final foundation of the universe, for there has to be some final foundation to everything, and what could be imagined better than the atom? Was the atom a piece of matter, however minute? Yes, it was. Why then could we not break it in two or imagine it as breakable? An irreverent question, the asking of which exposed us as ignoramuses, discourteous to our teachers and indocile to an awful Presence called Science in the name of which our teachers taught! We dared not commit such a blasphemy nor incur such reproach; so before the Atom we knelt like Buddhists of Ceylon before Gotama's sacred Tooth. Then all we had to do was to heap atoms together and shuffle them into various combinations —and in the twinkling of eye we had the universe and the universe all explained.

It was a tidy creed; and an immense amount of intellect of the first order spent itself in proving how tidy it was, how sufficient, how splendid a creation of the human mind. There remained of course a question or two in the unquiet heads which nothing can ever satisfy, but they did not seriously disturb the true believers. Such questions were: Why cannot the atom be broken up? The molecule which is a collection of atoms can be broken up; why then cannot its parts? And since force or energy must be added to or included in the atom if we are to have a universe not inert but in action, how did the force get there, and when it goes out of the atom how can the atom remain unchanged? And by what right can we say that the atom is the fundamental and original Ultimate? May it not be the Force which is the ultimate? Tormenting inquiries these, but we stood steadfast in faith and clung to our atoms as the inmost nucleus of matter and as containing the promise and potency of life and mind.

Well, although we have not got used to the blasting revolution yet, we now must admit that the creed is a mass of mythology and superstition. To-day it is blithering idiocy. The grandees and dictators of the intellectual life of the nineteenth century did not know what they were talking about, and the great inventors of that era who did marvelous tricks with matter had no idea what they were dealing with. Their dearest certainty is not far above the level of the theory that stars change their position in the sky because they are shoved along by angels. And what have the innovators and the iconoclasts to fetch forward in place of the atoms, the energies, the ether which as we knew them are dead and gone? Where, as an immortal question once asked on the floor of Congress, are we at? What is the cone of matter now? What the sequestered substance of the world? Let us listen, if we can continue breathing in so fine an air long enough to listen.

There are wave-packets of an electro-magnetic nature flying through space at varying frequencies. The wave-packets become coarse enough, or of a frequency low enough at certain spots to act upon our senses. But the "spot" at which they do so is not stationary, not a *punctum stans,* not a little region of quiescence; it is itself traveling at a lower velocity along with the waves. Moreover nothing carries or transmits the waves. All we can say of them in this weird cluster of apparent incantations is that they have a physical magnitude, a quantity represented or symbolized by the Greek letter ψ. But to this quantity or magnitude you must not give a physical interpretation; much less may you try to approach it by any picture in the sensuous imagination. For it is only a mathematical probability, the probability namely that at a certain world-point electro-magnetic waves will become observable to our senses. Matter then is electricity traveling in wave-packets carrying their locality with them; and these in turn become mathematical forms and probabilities not to be physically interpreted. Hence matter at least is not to be materially represented. It is refined away into an unknowable called electricity, and the electricity evaporates into mathematical forms. Space and time, the framework of matter, must be glued together as a fourth dimension, but even so, are inadequate to hold the elusive thing without distorting it and misleading us. Completely gone then are bulks and lumps and massive blocks. These gross appearances are only relative to our animal senses. In itself and apart from this low-relation, the final substance of things is a dance of energies footed to no measure that we can comprehend.

Upon these oracles let us venture a simple word or two. First, there is matter in the familiar meaning of the word only because we have bodily senses. Our senses are feeble and dull. We cannot see atoms or electricity. We cannot see force. We cannot hear the incessant whir of electrons. We cannot feel the rhythmic throb of electro-magnetic waves. The stuff of the world is absolutely beyond direct observation. So in our primitive immaturity we call a thing a tree and let it go at that, unaware that the object is actually a cluster of electric charges and of unimaginable millions of electrified particles or waves or particle-waves. Were our senses finer that object would be correspondingly finer. Hence to regard the distorting deliverances of our senses as revelations of the intimate and ultimate nature of the world, and upon these deliverances to build a theory of existence called Materialism, is nothing short of feeble-minded.

Next, the search for ultimate matter is hopeless. For even if we say that matter is a vortex in the ether, or a hump in space, or a concrescence of forms, or wandering electric charges, we are doing nothing but making vocal noises. If any one of these propositions or if all of them were true what would they tell us of the real thing? Nothing at all. They do not disclose an essence, they only amplify a vocabulary.

Furthermore there is a reason why the search is hopeless, a reason important to see. "What is matter?" is an intellectual question. It must therefore receive an intellectual answer. But nothing of the nature of matter is or can be an intellectual answer. As long as we remain on the level of matter, however fine and thin and small that matter may be, we cannot possibly satisfy a mental inquiry. The two things are of different kinds. So "What is matter?" can never be answered by offering us more matter or a new variety of matter. In any form, in any variety, it continues to be the thing we wished explained. What we want is not more of the thing to be explained, but an explanation. And there can be no explanation obviously except in mental terms. Therefore "What is matter?" if it is ever to be answered, can be answered only in ideal form ("ideal" here being taken of course as the adjective form of "idea"). In nothing other than thought can thought find rest. No other than an ideal satisfaction can satisfy Idea. No explanation can be a real explanation for mind unless it be of the nature of mind. Accordingly matter must be made a manifestation of Thought; else our thought could not be concerned about it. And that philosophical physics perceives this we see from its foremost men who are maintaining that matter at last has to be reduced to mathematical forms and refined away to equations which it requires our very highest thought to express. Thought manifests itself on many levels. The lowest one is matter. But even on the lowest there are peaks pointing to the higher and unintelligible without a Highest.

Finally from all this we may discern a new vindication for poetry, art, aspiration, and religion as revealers of reality. The senses are the most misleading of all transmitters of reality. Senses operate on surfaces. Conclusions drawn from them must ever be superficial. What then can pierce through surfaces and come closer to the indwelling secret and substance? Philosophical thought and intuitive insight—the minds that reason through and the souls that see through! When their sayings make our souls vibrant, uplift and enlarge them, complete the best that is in us, fulfill the prophecies that stir in us, and lay upon the head that holds the kingly mind a crown that fits it, they are true. For the soul's response is the first and last test of truth. The spirit's "Yea!" is the final and invincible demonstration. When therefore poet and saint penetrate the fog of materiality and illusion, clothe the world with beauty, fill its overarching vault with music, lift the sword of superhuman justice and in the firmament of being set the star of inextinguishable love, they are revealers of the Magnificence beyond. The rush of our souls to their announced vision proves it. And the decay of our souls if we reject it confirms the proof. And so at long last matter is not the world. It is the cradle-stage of the world. It is a foundation, hideous enough unless builded upon and beautiful only by participation in the whole structure, the rising stories of which are homes of an ever deepening loveliness of music, and the highest rooms of which are open to tender and heroic splendors poured forth from existence's undimmed morning and central Sun.

Shakespeare

So much of the Middle Ages is in him that he may almost be called the last bestowal of that epoch. For the Middle Ages were the most tragic-minded, the most dramatically vivid, the most imaginatively splendid of all eras of history. It had a sense of the mighty significance of Chaos, which is the persuasion that the course of the world runs onward under Forces vaster than they are kind and more powerful and not to be written down in our formulations. It had a feeling for the sublime individuality of existence, which only signifies that Destiny is past finding out and its way inscrutable, and that we are not poorer but richer for recognizing that it is so. It accepted retribution; it did not shrink from horror or pain; it was expectant of marvel, for the whole system of things was incalculable; it awaited Judgment, for beyond immoral man was a Supreme Moral Life. And of all this Shakespeare is an interpreting voice. A rational age can make nothing of him, so it expends its professionalized erudition upon the knowledge of his plays, the quality of his metaphors, and the state of his text. His soul and the world that fed his soul it can only regard as scandalous. To his ghosts, portents, soothsayers, witches, it can bring only a sterile intellectualism, asking the idiotic question: Does he mean us to take such nonsense literally? Before his terrifying insistence upon appalling and merciless retribution it can only stand jittering that there isn't any God and that human deeds are under an aimless and sanctionless drift of moral relativism. His ribaldry and bawdiness it lights upon, thinking that here is something that it can understand. But it cannot understand even this; for it ignores the difference between a central and morose contemplation of fierce animal lustiness, which is nowhere in Shakespeare, and fleshiness as a by-product of a wild farcical exuberance of the clownish and swinish side of man, which is everywhere in him.

Suggestive of the mediaeval spirit too is his understanding of human pettiness and transiency, of the flimsiness of exalted state, and of the crookedness of the natural man. But unlike it, and a quality all his own, is his reading of these great universals in individual characters. It was easier for him to see that individuals embody universals than that universals find determination in individuals. Hence his power of creating characters that are themselves alive, yet are animated with a life larger than their own moment, therefore alive forever.

Searching and inexorably probing into man's crooked heart he finds it mainly bad or foolish. And searching into the cold clear brain of pedants he finds it mainly malignant, and when not malignant, absurd. He had what religion calls a sense of sin, or what philosophers would call a tragic view of life. To a small mind a tragic view of life is dangerous, for it is near to pessimism. But a great mind perceives that pessimism is too easy a solution, as cynicism is too cheap a satisfaction. Shakespeare is therefore neither pessimist nor cynic.

His little land of England set in her silver sea evokes his patriot rapture. The blameless peace of forest and hamlet release the gladdest stirring of his most fragrant poetry. Then he bravely foots it with wholesome lads and lassies and with fairies of every degree of the elfin hierarchy. And the apparition of virginal innocence in a murky world clothes him with reverential awe. Last of all, the Higher Order beneath which men carry on their fantastic mummeries calls forth from him his stateliest eloquence. That Order avenges. No wheedling diverts its retributions; no pompousness, though it had at its back an army and on its head a crown, can find a cover so thick or a hole so deep as to escape the thunderbolt that blasts successful crime. Life as hurly-burly of man bipeds, plotting, cheating, defiling, is ridiculous; it is an evil dream, quintessential dust, and will not leave a trace behind. But life that has touched a starry region, clear of any spot, and life that has rebelled against the Avenger on high—that becomes invested with a loveliness superhuman, and with a tragic terror awful with prodigious doom. So in the abyss of his mind he apprehends the world's minuteness, and comprehends life's great magnificence. Lyric song and stately dirge.

The tragic intuition passes into spiritual insight, and as we close his crowded page we reflect that here is a man to whom much was laughable but nothing frivolous; to whom robust hilarity was natural but moral charlatanism impossible; to whom devious motives laid bare their windings but mystery kept its sombre curtain lowered; to whom the clean and simple heart was earth's most precious treasure, and blasting punishment for cold and deadly evil Heaven's fundamental law. To unfaith and unfaithfulness he speaks no word. With stony and conceited intellect he can have no communicable speech.

The product of a tradition too profound to be deluded by the humbug of mortality but too near to Reality to have nothing to revere, the Monarch of literature calls for the whole spirit of man to be his interpreter, and the purest vision of the soul to observe the pageanted evocations of his genius. He is for the mature but not for the modern mind.

www.ingramcontent.com/pod-product-compliance
Lightning Source LLC
Chambersburg PA
CBHW070546310726
48982CB00004B/847
9781512820096